Testimonials

"This book reveals the important role of an IT project coach to ensure a much higher rate of success in IT projects."
— Thomas K. Escher, former member of the group managing board at UBS

"Information Technology, as an engineering science, is a people business at heart. That's why we are carefully and constantly combining innovative minds with high performance technologists and banking business experts, on a global level."
— Stefan Arn, CIO Wealth Management, Head of WM IT and UBS Switzerland IT & Head Group Technology for Strategic Regulatory Initiatives, UBS AG

"This innovative and unique book examines the most important factor in IT project management: the human factor. It gives solid advice on how to steer any IT project through the challenges of its team members' interactions. The book should be required reading for every project manager who wants to gain inside into human psychology and how it determines his own and his teams' success or failure."
— Jörn Galka, Moderne IT, European Business Consultant

"I have met more people who perceive they have worked on failed projects, than on success stories. There is no doubt in my mind, that if their project sponsors had read this book first, the balance would tip strongly in the other direction."
—Dr. Graham King, CEO BRINE SA

"In *The Trillion Dollar IT Revolution*, Urs Milz provides an excitingly fresh perspective on managing IT projects to increase the likelihood of success in an arena in which failure coupled with loss of significant are far too common. He writes with insight and passion while meticulously outlining the steps businesses and corporations can take to join the revolution and in joining the IT revolution can generate an immediate boost to their bottom line."
—Tim Morrison, D.Min, ND, President,
Write Choice Services, Inc.

"This *Trillion Dollar IT Revolution* offers a great collection of insight and advice that supports business executives and business owners as well as IT managers."
—Dr. Richard Vögeli, Managing Partner at ensurAccess GmbH

"Excellent overview of Project Management—a good range of information and well presented key trends defining the future of IT business. I certainly like the emphasis on the IT project coaching approach."
—Dr. Thomas Rischbeck, Partner at IPT

"If you are a business owner or IT executive and want to realize your IT projects greatest potential leverage this book's compelling insights into how to bring IT projects forward to success."
—Dr. Andreas Maier, IT Problem Solver, CEO YOU-Hotels.com
(YOU International Limited)

"Coaching is a partnership with clients in a thought-provoking and creative process that inspires them to maximize their personal and professional potential. It is about supporting people in finding solutions they could not see before in a safe and trusting environment. This is of particular importance in a world of growing complexity and uncertainty in many workplaces today."

—Dr. Ernst Bechinie, ICF Master Certified Coach and author of
Secrets of Entrepreneurship

"It's not uncommon for projects to fail. Even if the budgets and schedules are met, one must ask 'did the project deliver the results and quality we expected?' During the course of managing a project, the project manager must monitor activities (and distractions) from many sources and directions. Complacency can easily set in. When this happens, the process of 'monitoring' breaks down. This is why the project manager must remain in control of a project and be aware of any activity which presents a risk of project failure. This book reveals the important and neutral role of the IT Project Coach to ensure extraordinary results of each IT project. It also reveals an extraordinary and unique way to produce optimized solutions in a highly competitive World."

—Raj Kosaraju, CIO at Maxil Technology Solutions, Inc.

the
Trillion
Dollar
IT
Revolution

the
Trillion
Dollar

IT REVOLUTION

a unique process to stop
enormous IT project failures

URS MILZ

media press association

Zürich

MEDIA PRESS ASSOCIATION
CH – 8000 Zürich
Switzerland
www.mediapressassociation.com

Ordering Information:
Quantity sales. Special discounts are available on quantity purchases by corporations, associations, and others. For details, contact the publisher at the address above.
Orders by trade bookstores and wholesalers. Please contact Lightning Source UK.

Cover design by Kathi Dunn, dunn-design.com
Interior design by Dorie McClelland, springbookdesign.com
Editing by Write Choice Services

First Edition, 2014
Printed by Lightning Source
ISBN 978-3-9524254-0-4

Disclaimer:
This book is sold with the understanding that the author and publisher are not engaged in rendering legal, accounting, or other professional services and advice. The information provided in this book is designed to provide helpful information on the subjects discussed. Every effort has been made to make this book as complete and as accurate as possible. However, there may be mistakes, both typographical and in content. Therefore, this book should be used only as a general guide and not as the ultimate source of the information contained herein. Furthermore, this book includes contact information for the authors, which has been furnished by them for the book. To the best of the publisher's knowledge, the contact information is accurate as of the printing date of this book. The author and publisher shall not be liable or responsible to any person or entity with respect to any loss or damage caused, or alleged to have been caused, directly or indirectly, by the information contained in this book. Although the author and publisher have made every effort to ensure that the information in this book was correct at press time, the author and publisher do not assume and hereby disclaim any liability to any party for any loss, damage, or disruption caused by errors or omissions, whether such errors or omissions result from negligence, accident, or any other cause.

In loving memory of Charly, my father

Contents

Acknowledgments

Without the significant contributions made by other people, this book would certainly not exist. I take this opportunity to express my profound gratitude and deep regards to the whole supporting team of John Eggen with special thanks to Janet Tingwald for her exemplary guidance, monitoring, coaching and constant encouragement throughout the course of this book production. In the end, I believe that the team that was chosen provides the perfect blend of knowledge and skills that went into authoring this book. I thank Anita Wuethrich for her illustrations and graphs, Dorie McClelland of Spring Book Design for her meticulous interior design, and Hobie Hobart and Kathi Dunn of Dunn+Associates for devoting their time toward professional project management and cover design for this book. I was very fortunate to have the support and assistance of a critical reader and editor, Dr. Tim Morrison. For their frankness and insights, I would like to thank Will Linssen and the entire team around Marshall Goldsmith. They all reinforced my faith in the potential of the project and their efforts helped to make this book complete. I couldn't have done it without you.

I also want to express a deep sense of gratitude to my wife, Fanny, for her cordial support, valuable information and guidance, which helped me in completing this book through various stages. Thank you, Fanny for standing beside me throughout my education and in writing this book. You have been my inspiration and motivation for continuing to improve my knowledge and move my education forward. You are my anchor.

I dedicate this book to her, to Fanny.

Lastly, I thank the Almighty, my parents and my sister, Beatrice, my whole family and friends for their constant encouragement without which this book would not have been possible. I hope that one day they can read this book and understand why I spent so much time in front of my computer.

Author's Note

I have tried to write this book in a gender-neutral language to avoid implicit or explicit references to gender. The language should be as inclusive as possible and not make any assumptions about professions belonging to one gender or the other. ITP coaches can be male or female. As I enjoy working with female colleagues and highly appreciate their professional skills, I would like to apologize if I was not successful throughout.

Foreword

Marshall Goldsmith

Thinkers 50 Top Ten Most Influential Management Thinker
in the World

Executive coaching is designed to support professional and personal development to the point of individual growth and enhanced performance. Coaches need to have a profound understanding of diversity and cultural awareness in the work place as well as the ability to adapt their coaching style to different situations. Urs Milz reveals in this book a unique insight into an innovative IT project coaching process.

The Stakeholder Centered Coaching approach I developed has proven to help successful people make positive lasting change in leadership behavior through using a methodology that is highly effective and time efficient.

Many other coaching approaches focus on leadership assessments and action planning, which result in a strong emphasis on awareness. Out of this framework, the leader intellectually understands that leadership change would generate a higher effectiveness. Though this step is critical at the outset of the coaching process, it often results in a long action list of good intentions that might not see the light of day. Stakeholder Centered Coaching takes the leadership change process into the leaders work environment, while the ITP coach approach brings a teamwork enhancement process into IT projects. Stakeholders can provide important and insightful suggestions for behavioral change that would help the leader and IT project members to become more effective on the job. The Stakeholder Centered Coaching process includes a strong emphasis on action implementation and follow through. This helps to make change stick and creating more effective leadership behaviors and habits. Urs' vision of the ITP coaching process focuses on establishing positive behaviors and habits to create outstanding results in IT project management.

The role of the coach has always been to improve the performance of others as it applies to sports, art or business. If leaders are to improve in their own practice of leadership, they need leverage. A coach adds value to the degree that the coach can help the leaders and teams gain leverage. Helping speed up the learning curve and turning that learning into productive behavior is why a coach is important.

When a person is asked to focus on a topic so personal as his or her own behavior, it is often useful to have an objective, experienced and qualified pair of eyes to assist in interpreting feedback and suggestions. This is where a coach adds enormous value. The coach's perspective helps further develop the individual's self-awareness.

Successful people welcome getting ideas that are aimed at helping them achieve their goals. The ITP coaching process is focusing back on positive teamwork to make people enjoy their work and achieve highly motivated their targets.

The independent role of an ITP coach as described in this book offers all requirements for a successful executive coaching to an IT project team. While executive coaching is a top-down approach, the ITP coaching process acts bottom-up. Those two approaches strongly integrate stakeholders and thus form an excellent complementary to the entire company's success.

All truths are easy to understand once they are discovered;
the point is to discover them.
Galileo Galilei (1564–1642)

1

Introduction

The Trillion Dollar IT Revolution presents a revolutionary idea with well-defined processes and procedures to significantly increase the success rate for IT projects.

Studies indicate that 30–70% of all information technology (IT) projects fail. Curiously, projects do not fail because of the technology or the choice of a procedure.

Projects fail due to:

- A lack of information given to the project team;
- Poor communication among the team members or between other groups and the team;
- Lack of confidence in the project among the team members assigned to the project;
- Lack of confidence by management in the team's ability to solve problems.

A study conducted by the University of Mannheim concerning successful IT projects discovered that IT teams whose projects were successful worked fewer hours than other IT projects that were not successful. In other words, long hours and overtime does not contribute to and certainly does not guarantee project success.

From a financial perspective, the average company lists "at risk—projects" totaling $74 million every year.

The huge gap between projects initiated and projects successfully completed in IT project management begs to be addressed.

The primary purpose of this book is to convince IT managers that each IT project needs a coach. The dedicated role of an ITP coach dramatically increases the likelihood of success for IT projects.

By following the advice of a notable, "big thinker," I attempt to make the vision behind the ITP coach approach very easy to understand:

> *The only rational way of educating is to be an example—*
> *if one can't help it, a warning example.*
> Albert Einstein (from a letter to Irene Freuder, 20.11.1932)

To implement this revolution, this book presents a process to bring together ITP coaches in a collective learning group. In chapter 8, I discuss the core idea of creating an ITP coaches network comprised of a community of IT specialists and good coaching professionals. This community will grow together, building and certifying a new profession: the IT project coach.

In chapter 2, I discuss the strong need to leverage leadership and communication which are the main project oriented and networking tasks of an ITP coach. This includes consideration of communication challenges in the globalized labor market. Other topics are the challenge of choosing the right tool from the wealth of project management tools and different studies and reports about the todays' challenges.

Chapter 3 addresses the specific tasks of an ITP coach which, when implemented in an IT project, generate success by effectively using collective learning.

Chapter 4 describes how companies can increase success rates through motivated employees and by generating better understanding among members of the project team. Also found in this chapter are the ways in which business coaching and ITP coaching differ and the significance of those differences. Chapter 4 closes with a look at values, purpose and goal setting.

Methods to multiply success rates of IT projects while helping people experience more satisfaction at work are at the core of chapter 5. We learn the importance of building trust within a project team. Chapter 5 also challenges managers to make effective use of the 80-20 rule and to recognize that ITP coaching improves project management.

Chapter 6 leads the reader through issues relevant to:

- Global and local factors that affect the labor market, methods and goals;
- Challenges that arise because project members have different ways to express themselves;
- Cost pressures in a rapidly changing environment;
- Global labor market exploitation for self-interest;
- Power and success factors that lead to current challenges;
- Communication issues in big programs;
- Projects involving innovation and competitive modes;
- Challenges arise because of matters inherent to the system.

Chapter 7 discusses matters specific to team building, particularly instilling positive qualities to motivate the team to work with deep commitment for project success. The steps to creating an adaptable system that relies on focused teamwork to address current and future challenges and then drawing upon collective learning theory to consistently attain success are the lessons taught in chapter 8.

Chapter 9 topics focus on the core idea of the advantages experienced with a strong network and team network. Also discussed is the critical importance of network member principles' to establish and maintain a code of ethical conduct.

How to build trust as the foundation of the ITP coaches network is the primary topic of chapter 10. The chapter closes with a look at the Pool approach and its influence on the world of employment and the importance of strategic alliances.

Chapter 11 describes how to identify and send a person of trust to become a part of the network. Additionally the reader learns the several positive effects of the two-step approach to becoming a member of the ITP coach association.

2

The Stunning Truth:
Why Half of All IT Projects Fail

Communication and leadership transformation

A stunning truth is that over the decades of IT projects, more than half of all IT projects fail. Failure occurs not because of technical challenges but from communication issues.

Various studies indicate that in order for IT project teams to achieve project goals (build success stories), IT projects need to be more intentional in creating and leveraging effective leadership and communication within IT project teams. This book establishes a unique and sustainable IT coaching approach in order to significantly increase success rates of IT projects while simultaneously enabling those involved in IT projects to experience more fulfillment in their work.

Stakeholder Centered Coaching by Marshall Goldsmith (SCC-MG) focuses on enabling successful people to lead more effectively through long-term change in leadership behavior. The Stakeholder Centered Coaching process guarantees measurable leadership growth.

The Trillion Dollar IT Revolution seeks to do the same in the IT project arena.

In the time since the global financial crisis of 2007–2008, organizations have learned that they can get along with fewer employees. After downsizing, survivors found themselves filling the roles of two or more colleagues laid off or outsourced as part-time contractors. As a result, many executives who formerly had administrative support staff have been given additional productivity responsibilities and told to fend for themselves. Unfortunately, for some of the managers, their skill gaps have become visible because of the lack of their core competencies. An excellent executive assistant with strong communication skills is difficult to replace by tools.

As the Stakeholder Centered Coaching approach supports leaders in becoming successful, the ITP coach approach brings to awareness the fields of challenges and supports the IT project team in addressing those challenges.

In addition, the ITP coach approach equips the IT project teams with the necessary tools to effectively address the leadership and communication concerns. The primary issues center around making the important decisions, shaping the organizational culture and affecting a positive communication climate. Mastering these primary issues contributes to generating a solid image of and future for the company and influences in a beneficial way employee attitudes and perceptions.

Part of the job of the ITP coach is to monitor the perceptions the IT project team members have of the project. Then, based upon the collective perceptions, the ITP coach will make necessary adjustments to maintain successful leadership and supportive communication.

You will find much more about this conscious, authentic and empathetic approach to support employees, management and stakeholders in the following chapters.

Tasks of an ITP coach

Specifically developed course programs will be designed to ensure the high professional qualification of an ITP Coach.

Drawing upon my professional expertise in IT Project Management to multinationals in which I helped them save money and time and significantly reduce personnel burn-out, I submit that the primary responsibilities of an ITP coach are:

- Accompanying IT projects from inception through development of the business case;
- Participating in selective meetings—within the project team, as well as with stakeholders;
- Coaching sessions with all "key members" of the project team;
- Generating field reports on project management and stakeholders;
- Ensuring project managers and team members understand and grow from "Lessons Learned" scenarios.

Networking tasks of an ITP coach are to:

- Provide strong supervision by and for other ITP coaches in the network;
- Commit to engaging in collective learning processes for personal and network wide improvement through sharing stories of projects on which they have worked; Strengthen bonds among themselves one to one and collectively so network members are eager to learn from each other and enhance their skills and knowledge;
- Take jobs in different projects and companies, ensuring a neutral role of the ITP coach;
- Participate and prepare speeches in regular network meetings of the ITP coach association;
- Be certified as an ITP coach and assist others to be certified.

The book discusses the importance of the neutral role of the ITP Coach which is crucial in guaranteeing the success of an IT project. Just as a pilot helps big ships to enter the harbor safely, an ITP Coach assists all project members to build a guaranteed success with the highest possible motivation.

I reveal in this book a process to improve IT Project Management which will lead to considerable monetary savings. Above all, *The Trillion Dollar IT Revolution* seeks to make IT work more enjoyable by shifting the focus from Human Capital to Human Beings. *The Trillion Dollar IT Revolution* presents a holistic vision of leadership, communication and success in today's IT world.

The tasks of an ITP coach discussed in this book provide an overview of the role of an ITP coach and how such a coach will address the challenges that are about to be discussed. The importance of the strong supporting skills of an ITP coach is discussed throughout the book.

Global market challenges

Changes in today's IT project world are crucial. Because of the globalized labor market, the communication challenges are greater than ever. Staffs work with different language and cultural backgrounds in constantly-changing project teams. Just as all big ships who want to enter a foreign harbor anywhere in the world need a pilot, we need a good, solid, worldwide network of ITP coaches to support IT projects wherever they occur and regardless of the team's make up.

Teri Okoro and Zuzana Botkova, in a survey of APM Knowledgeshare on the 13th of May 2010 with the title "The Progression of Women in Project Management," concluded:

- Emotional intelligence and soft skills are what make the difference in PM;
- Individuality and personality are key;
- Importance of long-term career vision and goals.

Chapter 9 discusses the important advantages derived by understanding and using emotional intelligence throughout the project development.

As individuality and personality are key, this takes on even greater significance in the global labor market in which different cultures mix.

An unexpected outcome from the recent global financial crisis is that organizations have learned that they can get along with fewer employees. Because of this, those who remain employed tend to lack confidence that they will receive long-term work assignments. This triggers the realization for the need to have long-term career goals and vision.

In the coaching sessions with the IT project members, the ITP coach has the opportunity to address the anxieties. Then the most important part is to take action. Drawing upon processes from the Stakeholder Centered Coaching and combining them with the ITP coach approach, the ITP coach provides support for employees to re-anchor their confidence and loyalty in the global market place.

We live in a world that has a number of different communications infrastructures in place, many of which are global. While the Internet is the most universal and recent of all global communications solutions, a misuse of this platform often takes place in the working environment. The Internet is a global network of interconnected computers, which is also integrated into digital assistants, mobile phones and gaming devices. On one hand the modern business needs this communication platform; on the other hand, there is always the possibility that employees will devote too much time to games, texting and other online distractions at the expense of moving projects along.

The Internet makes possible ongoing cross-cultural communications. The ITP coaches network can track how people from differing cultural backgrounds communicate among themselves, and how they endeavor to communicate across cultures. The network shares this information among the members so each is better prepared as an ITP coach to communicate effectively with, between, and among team members.

Effective e-mail communication is very important in globalized business. But one must determine when an e-mail is and is not an efficient way of communicating and then use e-mails that successfully convey your message to your intended audience. An employee in a small company may become engaged in interactions with a big multinational company. Occasionally an e-mail will be generated that shows hundreds of cc. The employee from the small company might think he needs to cc everyone in reply. That is not necessarily correct and to do so would seem amusing. The impact, though, could lead to a huge data-trash.

Miscommunication can easily occur when people have different expectations about the e-mails that they send and receive. The use of capital and small letters in e-mails can create problems. In some setting CAPITALS SUGGEST THAT THE WRITER IS SHOUT-ING; where as in others, using CAPITALS is understood as a way to emphasize a point. Understanding e-mail protocol can help to avoid misunderstandings.

Another example is that some people regard e-mail as a rapid and informal form of communication to say "hello" or to ask a quick question. However, others view e-mail as a more convenient way to transmit a formal message. Such people may consider an informal e-mail rude or unprofessional.

In each of these situations, the ITP coach can provide appropriate information and protocol concerning the use of e-mails within and among project team members. The insights that an ITP coach offers about the uses of e-mail and e-mail protocol are very useful and reduce the likelihood of team members offending others through misunderstandings innocently generated in e-mails.

Shared drives, also known as network drives, are typically used to store and share content. The use of shared drives poses challenges because project members may store content that includes private information or other even inappropriate material. Think of parking restrictions in the community in which you live. Unless there are local parking restrictions giving a right to a particular space, citizens do not have automatic rights to a parking space on a public road. However, they do have a right of access to their drive. If there is a shared drive, then each person has a right of access and neither should block the drive. This applies to shared drives in the IT world. No one should create hindrances or blocks that prevent others from accessing the drives. Again, the ITP coach can help to raise awareness of challenges.

Although we have a global platform, we do not have a global culture; cultural awareness is very important in mixed project teams.

Wealth of management tools challenges

IT projects are blessed and burdened because of the wealth of project management tools. We have so many good Project Management tools to choose from that we tend to lose sight of the project goals and focus instead on using the right tools, the perfect tools and that pursuit becomes a limitation.

Done is better than perfect.
Facebook COO Sheryl Sandberg

The quote from Facebook leader Sheryl Sandberg reflects the challenge for multinational IT projects, especially in financial IT where the reputation for damage provoked by imperfect IT systems is legendary. It's crucial to find symmetry between a perfect execution and a "done is better than perfect" solution. The ITP coach is equipped with all skills to balance such challenging decisions.

Clearly defined actions derived from appropriate management tools support the 20/80 rule known as the Pareto principle. ITP managers must be aware of this as it impacts the overall process of the project. The impact of the Pareto principle is described in more detail in chapter 5.

Regardless of the Project Management tools in play, the ITP coach can be deployed in all IT projects, all over the world. In every setting, the alignment is action-and-solution-oriented.

There are so many benchmarks to fulfill in the IT business and just as many tools are available to comply with these benchmarks. But if half of IT projects fail, all this effort is for nothing. In spite of all the risk management units continuously controlling and reviewing benchmarks and tools used, half of all IT projects worldwide still fail.

What if someone could walk you through a process, step by step to significantly increase your project success rate, would that interest you?

My answer is that I have that process. I have that information. I know the steps to save you time and money while significantly increasing your success rate and profitability.

> *If you are not prepared to be wrong,*
> *you'll never come up with anything original.*
> Sir Ken Robinson

IT projects are sufficiently prepared to be wrong and it's time now to come up with a powerful ITP coach approach that makes things right.

Currently, IT project management tools are monitored and controlled by a top down approach. The ITP coaching establishes a stronger connection and communication to the base. As a bottom up approach, the ITP coach keeps the management and stakeholders informed on the progress. This 360 degree step by step approach is the positive answer to your painful question and a powerful way to success.

Employee feedback should be given as frequently as possible. Constructive feedback is crucial to employee motivation, satisfaction and retention. Feedback about project management tools takes place through the annual performance review forms and ensuing discussions, but also informally through ongoing conversations and coaching. The ITP coach approach is an additional formal feedback to improve the power of a management tool.

Success story of the ITP coaches network

The network of the ITP Coach Association will be the safe harbor. The benefit of the collective learning and shared information that emerges from association members will grow with the number of ITP coaches working on projects. As information and experiences are shared, the success of IT projects will also increase dramatically!

Another comment by Sir Ken Robinson emphasizes this:

"You cannot predict the outcome of human development. All you can do is like a farmer—create the conditions under which it will begin to flourish."

In their network the ITP coaches work together in a well cross-linked community. Together they develop their own skill sets by bringing their diverse project experiences to the association and by enhancing their own skills through collective supervision. Chapters 9 and 10 detail how the network and the framework assist the ITP coach.

An ITP coach can share with management specific examples of how individual employees perform. Supplied with specific information, management praises their employees on doing a great job.

Often it's easy to detect that the project team is doing a good job, especially when innovation is required. Listen carefully. You will hear the talk. The need for innovation is sometimes a huge challenge. Turning to outsourced specialists seems to be the only chance. The ITP coaches network is pure innovation and from this background, it is also easy to discover them in the project team.

Through close contact and regular coaching with the project team, the ITP coach is able to address all challenges quickly and directly as they surface. As the ITP coach expands his own network, all involved IT projects will be part of this success story and will flourish too. More about all the great advantages of IT project coaching is found in chapter 3.

A basket full of challenges

We know that stakeholder, IT and project managers have their personal opinions about the origins of IT project failures. Even very experienced project managers are confronted with challenging situations. There are no two identical combinations of IT project scope, objective and/or environment. Statistics and surveys attempt to bring some objectivity in assessing the origins of IT project failures.

Effective data and information management is a very important matter for many organizations. The quantity of digital information in the world is increasing tenfold every five years, and organizations are having a difficult time managing this data and keeping it secure.

In a study conducted by Virginia Commonwealth University, fewer than 10 percent of organizations use documented processes to manage their data, and fewer than one in three organizations claim confidence in their own data. In the next chapter a subchapter is dedicated to actual information challenges.

Why projects fail: an opinion from Greg Martin (Parthenon Consultancy Ltd.) based on his experience in the following definition, some reasons and problems.

Definition of project success and failure

Projects are successful if they deliver the required result within schedule and within budget.

If any one or more of these criteria are not met then the project has failed. Many project failure statistics have been published, and they mostly indicate that more than half of all projects fail.

Some reasons for project failure

Understanding why aspects of a project can fail is the key to understanding what needs to be done in order to improve the chances that a project will be successful.

- Lack of executive support and stakeholder involvement;
- Conflicts between stakeholders;
- Failure to produce or update the Business Case;
- Unrealistic time or resource estimates;
- Unclear or changing goals and objectives;
- Scope creep or feature creep;
- Lack of a change control system;
- Poor or absent quality control;
- Lack of adequate planning;
- Failure to communicate and act as a team;
- Poor or no requirements definition;
- Lack of required resources;
- Staff with inappropriate skills.

Problems with middle and senior management attitudes

Middle and senior management attitudes that can contribute to project failure include:

- Political decisions to exclude some stakeholders from consultation;
- Appointment of a hard-hitting "firefighter" project manager to a project that requires a strategic thinker;
- Lack of knowledge of how to implement culture change;
- Petty disputes between senior individuals or departments cause stagnation;
- Lack of feedback of failure warning signals from staff due to a culture of management by edict;
- Failure to have or to communicate the business case leads to a lack of direction;
- Viewing project management as merely the ability to use a project planning software tool, whereas it is the orchestration of human resources to capture requirements, plan the project, report progress, control risks and formally accept what the project delivers;

- Budget restrictions limit the upfront investment of time, causing downstream costs when correcting problems that were avoidable.

Project management is primarily a philosophy of people management. It is not just a technique, software tool or an administrative function.

True Project Management requires an "active" manager, not a "reactive" one.

To find out more about Greg and Parthenon, go to http://www.parthenon.uk.com/project-failure.htm.

The Standish Group's Chaos Report (2003) showed—in comparison to its previous findings—that over the past decade, a greater number of projects did achieve a successful outcome. Yet the report also revealed that two out of three present-day projects usually fail. This paper examines twelve reasons why projects fail, reasons that the author identified through roundtable discussions with IT professionals and business executives.

The Chaos Report 1995 has been conducted among 365 IT managers from companies of various sizes and in various economic sectors. Key findings are shown in the next illustration.

Please find more statistical information on:

http://www.it-cortex.com/Stat_Failure_Cause.htm#The Chaos Report (1995)

In the Bull Survey (1998) a key finding is that bad communications between relevant parties is a major cause of project failure.

A study on large scale IT Projects from McKinsey & Company in conjunction with the University of Oxford 2012 finds that the well-known problems with IT Project Management persist. Among the key findings quoted from the report:

"Seventeen percent of large IT projects go so badly that they can threaten the very existence of the company"

Project impaired factors

		% of the responses
1.	Incomplete requirements	13.1 %
1.	Lack of user involvement	12.4 %
1.	Lack of resources	10.6 %
2.	Unrealistic expectations	9,9 %
1.	Lack of executive support	9.3 %
1.	Changing requirements & specifications	8.7%
1.	Lack of planning	8.1 %
1.	Didn't need it any longer	7.5 %
1.	Lack of IT management	6.2 %
1.	Technology illiteracy	4.3 %
1.	Other	9.9 %

Illustration 1: Project impaired factors similar to chaos report

Key findings

57% Bad communication between parties

39% Lack of planning of scheduling resources & activities

35% No quality control

34% Milestones not being met

29% Inadequate co-ordination of resources

26% Costs getting out of hand

20% Mismanagement of progress

17% Overall poor management

13% Supplier skills overstretched

12% Supplier under resources

11% Insufficient measurable outputs

4% Supplier people not consistent

Illustration 2: Key findings of the Bull survey (1998)

and

"On average, large IT projects run 45 percent over budget and 7 percent over time, while delivering 56 percent less value than predicted."

More facts and figures why projects fail on: http://calleam.com/WTPF/?page_id=1445.

In the KPMG Canada Survey (1997) the key findings emerged that poor project planning, weak business case and lack of top management involvement and support consistently lead to project failure.

It's really nice to know all this and to have all these findings in lessons- learned reports, but how better would it be to react in the current situation. An ITP coach has all the means and the neutral role to do this.

To underline the critical situation without the ITP coach approach, I have more statistical material about challenges in today's IT world:

A study of GENECA on March 2011 revealed that among 600 respondents, up to 75% of business and IT executives anticipate their software projects will fail. Interviews of people closely involved in software development projects found the following key message:

"Fuzzy business objectives, out-of-sync stakeholders, and excessive rework."

Meant that 75% of project participants have lack of confidence that their projects will succeed. A truly stunning 78% of respondents reported that:

"Business is usually or always out of sync with project requirements."

Like in a self-fulfilling prophecy, management predictions stated above become true either directly or indirectly.

These soft factors can hardly be fixed through specific PM changes, and are usually more feelings than concretely verifiable challenges. Because of these factors, it is even more important that an ITP coach accompany the IT project and determines appropriate actions and reactions in any current situation.

An October 2008 IBM survey of 1,500 change management executives in the success / failure rates of "change" projects finds:

- Only 40% of projects met schedule, budget and quality goals;
- Best organizations are 10 times more successful than worst organizations;
- Biggest barriers to success are listed as people factors: Changing mindsets and attitudes—58%. Corporate culture—49%. Lack of senior management support—32%;
- Underestimating the complexity of the project listed as a factor in 35% of projects.

In July 2008 the United States Government Accountability Office showed in a review of federally funded technology projects:

- 413 of 840 (49%) federally funded IT projects are either poorly planned, perform poorly or both.

This last statement illustrates the importance that the ITP coach approach can have if implemented in private industry as well as for states all over the world.

All these statistics have one thing in common: the problem areas are manifold and many IT projects fail. The need for action is immense and recognized at all management levels.

The areas that generate the most pain are:

- Communication challenge—in the globalized world of work, people with different languages, different ways of life and cultures come together;
- Leadership challenge—the present power structures will gradually lose their momentum, or be transformed into non-hierarchical organic structure in the team.

A 2011 IT Project Success Rates Survey was performed during the last two weeks of October and there were 178 respondents. The survey was announced in Scott Ambler's October 2011 DDJ column, DDJ blog, on the Ambysoft announcements list, Scott Ambler's Twitter feed, and several LinkedIn discussion forums (IASA, TDWI, Enterprise Architecture Network, Greater IBM connection, and Considerate Enterprise Architecture Group).

The survey results are summarized in Scott Ambler's November 2011 Dr. Dobb's Journal column "How Successful are IT Projects, Really?" on the web page: http://www.ambysoft.com/surveys/success2011.html.

Some findings include:

- As you can see in illustration 3, Agile and Iterative project teams have statistically identical success rates;
- As you can see in illustration 3, ad-hoc project teams (no defined process) and traditional project teams have lower success rates that agile/iterative project teams;
- Illustration 4 compares the effectiveness of the five paradigms for delivering in a timely manner, for providing good ROI, for delivering value to the stakeholders, and for producing a quality product;
- When it comes to time/schedule, 20% prefer to deliver on time according to the schedule, 26% prefer to deliver when the system is ready to be shipped, and 51% say both are equally important;
- When it comes to ROI, 15% prefer to deliver within budget, 60% prefer to provide good return on investment (ROI), and 25% say both are equally important;
- When it comes to stakeholder value, 4% prefer to build the system to specification and 80% prefer to meet the actual needs of stakeholders, and 16% say both are equally important;
- When it comes to quality, 4% prefer to deliver on time and on

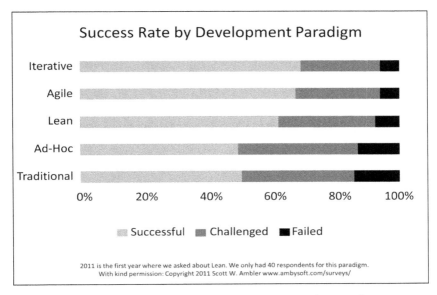

Illustration 3: Perceived IT project success rates by paradigm

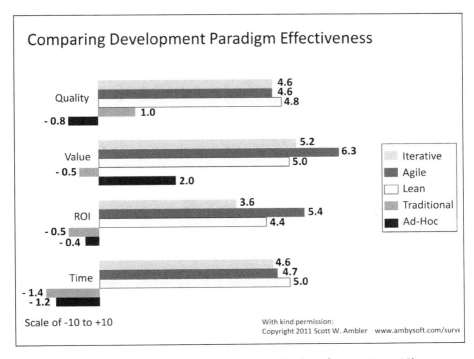

Illustration 4: Success factors by paradigm (Scale is from -10 to +10)

budget and 57% prefer to deliver high-quality, easy-to-maintain systems, and 40% say both are equally important;
- Only 12% of respondents indicated that their definition of success on their most recent project included all three of delivering according to schedule, within budget, and to the specification (answers where both was indicated were included in this calculation).

The following chapters describe the specific steps to achieve in order to experience continuous self-improvement that is cost effective for any company. A certified ITP coach is the critical piece in the process.

Recapitulation of the themes of this chapter:
- Strong need to leverage leadership and communication;
- Main project oriented and networking tasks of an ITP coach;
- Communication challenges because of the globalized labor market;
- The challenge about the wealth of project management tools;
- The advantage of the ITP coaches network to let flourish your success;
- Different studies and reports about the todays challenges.

3

The Power and Purpose for Success Stories in IT Project Coaching

Grow together through collective learning

The ITP coach brings a new framework to project management and out of this new framework and its process will emerge highly motivating success stories of IT project coaching. The stories will speak of the challenges encountered and conquered, of paths taken that proved to be wrong but because of the way ITP coaching functions course corrections were quickly made and the projects moved on to completion.

To begin to build these success stories and the network, interested companies will identify qualified, reliable people from among their employees and send them for training to become certified in the ITP coaches network. These confident, trained individuals become the foundation for the ITP coaching network. These individuals share their stories with each other and with all future certified coaches. The circle expands. The collective knowledge grows. Companies benefit immeasurably. You can download at www.itp-coach.com/sk a statement by Sir Ken Robinson in which he suggests that the collective learning approach will revolutionize our society. This collective learning approach leads also to a truly motivating, powerful and highly effective Network for the ITP coach. Chapter 8 (Subchapter: Team power by collective learning) explains in detail this revolutionary approach.

Companies who send an individual for the ITP coach training benefit immediately. Their representative gains new insight on ITP managing and becomes a part of an effective and active network that will always be available for each other to share new insights into success. Pragmatically, there is a dramatic lessening of the risk for budget losses because of a failed project. As the concept and value of an ITP coach gains acceptance, more companies and individuals will seek training and certification. Each individual adds to the "data bank" of information and best practices. The ongoing collective learning among certified ITP coaches constantly increases the value and reputation of an ITP coach. This reputation of solid knowledge and success encourages multinationals to trust in the ITP coaching approach and to participate in the certification process. Of course, this strengthens the probability for success with IT projects. Using the ITP coaches network with your company's IT projects reduces overall risk, increases the likelihood of success and generates more return to the company's bottom line.

With any new building technology there is a period of implemental learning required. For this new ITP coaches network the implementation period is supported by the collective learning approach and the collective power or wisdom of the team. In the network and together with all the individual skillsets, the output and speed of implementation for the success story will be multiplied. It's important to train the mindset of the ITP coaches to recognize and utilize all these opportunities.

In a short 5-minute video http://www.youtube.com/watch?v=6-gC8pWIn6k Julio Olalla explains the importance that the view of an observer brings to collective learning truth.

I describe in this book different concepts to demonstrate the vision that increasing the success rate of IT projects has a positive effect such that IT people consistently experience more enjoyment from their work. In a holistic understanding of a new theory, the conscious realignment of the mindset is supported by the collective.

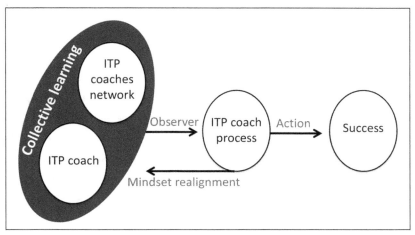

Illustration 5: Feedback system of the success story

The drawing illustrates this feedback to the ITP coach for a readjustment of the observer view and an aligned action from the approach to a guaranteed success.

The ITP Coach receives continuous feedback from the network as driven through the collective learning. The ITP coach realigns his approach as necessary as determined by the mindset view of the observer(s) (the ITP coaches network). The observer(s) comments are based on the outcomes generated by the action. From this point of view as an observer, the ITP coach approach takes action to success. A success story is born!

ITP Coach tasks to success

If the success story is well established, the following tasks of the ITP coaches will revolutionize project management:

1. Accompanying IT projects from the development of the business case

In the current project management scenario, certain core meetings are set. At the beginning of a project these meetings take place between IT and business in order to create the business case. The ITP coach has to participate in these core meetings to get an overview of the project and the core communication and leading principles. The content and outcomes of these meetings is of utmost importance because potential challenges in the project should be recognized as early as possible. Current practice suggests that too frequently the initial discussions take place without IT involvement.

A core concept of *The Trillion Dollar IT Revolution* is that the ITP coach works in different projects and companies in order to present a neutral and generalist position. Thus, project weakness points can be more easily recognized, addressed and eliminated.

2. Selective meeting participation—within the project team, as well as with stakeholders

If the business case is approved, periodic team meetings are held in the project. Depending on the status of the project, the coach will selectively participate in these meetings.

In addition, the ITP coach also participates in meetings of the steering committee and other stakeholders.

This periodic meeting attendance brings to the coach a good overview of the project. This results in a clear overview of the objectives. The goals in turn are tracked periodically by the coaching feedback from the project team. This improves the understanding of the objectives and delivers greater assurance of total project achievement.

3. Coaching sessions with all "key roles" of the project team

In the coaching sessions, personal goals are specified. Possible discrepancies to the project objectives can be clearly recognized.

Through the implementation of coaching ethics, processes and standards, ITP coaches will more readily recognize potential problems or unconscious patterns between team members and then address those matters. This coaching approach eliminates conflicts before they become destructive.

The persons involved in the coaching sessions also get the feeling that the human element is placed back into an important part of the project success. It also strengthens the self-confidence of employees and their motivation to participate on the project and be a part of the team's success. In this environment, some challenges will not only be solved but also will be changed into important advantages.

As IT projects become even more complex, certain patterns can be identified by the observer role of the ITP coach. Additionally the individual coaching sessions the ITP coach has with each team member facilitates team member's acquiring deeper insight into the challenges of the project.

4. Enhancing the efficiency and effectiveness of application development

Many application-development organizations need a metric in place to measure productivity. With every metric emanates some level of overhead to calculate and track that metric. Sometimes the overhead has proved higher than the benefits afforded by them.

The ITP coach works with excellent skills to monitor metrics. The ITP coach shares the observations in the network where the newest and most innovative trends are discussed among the coaches. The ITP coach then implements the suggestions that surfaced during the discussions. These network discussions can also assist the ITP coach in what to look for as the next potential group of challenges. The ITP coach in turn shares these insights not only with the project team but also with project management and stakeholders. All segments offer ideas and suggestions on how to react to and deal with the challenges when they appear.

5. Field reports on project management and stakeholders

The findings from the observations of the ITP coach are reported periodically to the project management and stakeholders. Thus, stakeholders will gain an additional and targeted survey of the project.

The reports of the ITP coach can also be synchronized with the project status report.

Special feedback sessions can be placed situationally.

6. Ensuring "Lessons Learned" scenarios

After completion of the project, a lesson learned meeting is set up by the coach in conjunction with the PMO (project management office).

In this lessons-learned meeting, important lessons for other projects are articulated and recognized. This knowledge base strengthens all stakeholders in all subsequent projects.

7. Summation and perfecting of all these characteristics

In a single company, the duties of an ITP coach are very helpful and supportive. The biggest benefit gained is that the coach is used in several companies and different projects simultaneously. In addition, all of these success factors are amplified by the continuous connection to the ITP coaches network.

On the internet at www.itpcoach.com/01 can be found actual examples and more detailed information about this revolutionary approach and the neutral and systematic observation and monitoring of IT projects.

Let information support this world

Timely and updated information of employees concerning the status of IT projects is critical. Showing the continual progress and growing success of IT projects testifies to the importance of an ITP coach. This person keeps things moving! Implementing a process to consistently share status reports ensures the trustworthiness of information and the credibility of the project. Employees within the project as well as those outside of the specific project recognize that when information flows from a specific source it is truthful.

This process also provides for the protection of whistleblowers.

Historically "whistle blowing" has emphasized concepts of personal responsibility and accountability. This has been long accepted in principle, but rarely implemented. Employees may not be able to deal with the flood of information from the media. Something may not sound right or "feel" right. How can the employee be sure? What if an employee engages in whistleblowing and later realizes that was a bad decision? Having a recognized conduit for information establishes a trust level among the company and its employers.

A number of countries have enacted whistleblower statutes that protect employees who disclose various types of misconduct or incompetence. These statutes are impressive not only because of their number, but also because they have been adopted in legal and cultural contexts seemingly inconsistent with those contexts. In the global labor market, the mixing of cultures is so intense that it is strongly recommended to use the assistance of a coach to provide clarity on rules. When the ITP coach and the project team members meet for discussions of the project, collectively they can address and resolve outstanding issues.

The ITP coach approach prevents a loss of important information and the publication of confidential data can be avoided. It also supports having the "right" information when it's required and essential.

Data and information management is the responsibility of your whole company; it affects everyone in your organization. It can control how good you connect with your customers, how safe your data is, and how aware your customers are. Information management determines how efficiently everyone can meet their goals and achieve performance metrics. The ITP coach is a very helpful support for this communication vision.

Effective information management is very important and it should be given serious, long-term attention from everyone from the management down to the newest employee on the team. Keep in mind that renovating an existing information system or synchronizing your databases can be an enormous cost, and a difficult project that could take many months or even years to implement. However, you can take the ITP coach approach to improve data management for your team, and for your organization and update systems more quickly.

By listing the frustrations, bottlenecks, and inefficiencies that the IT project members experience regularly with information and data availability, the ITP coach receives solid feedback that allows the ITP coach to readjust your data and information management. With all the inefficiencies, and security points that the ITP coach has identified, the IT department is able to fix some of these issues, or to suggest new ways to access the data needed. This important feedback can also be considered during system upgrades and redesigns.

A creative, organic and successful world

As IT technology is subject to organic growth, IT projects also need flexibility in order to meet project needs and requirements. In business and even in our lives, we favor engaging in linear processes and linear thinking: step A leads to step B which leads to step C and so on.

Creativity expert Sir Ken Robinson has studied linear thinking and educational processes and has derived some very interesting findings. In linear processes, one starts from a specific point continues through a certain path, and if everything is done correctly, one arrives at the end. We see this in education all the time. As an example, when one undertakes computer science education, one begins with the introductory courses, moves on to the intermediate courses and then the high level courses. One passes course finals, receives grades, graduates and now is ready to participate in IT projects. But life is not necessarily linear; life is rather organic. And being able to escape linear thinking and processing in favor of more creative, organic thinking serves companies and organizations better.

In IT, there are always new and different process models and development philosophies such as the Waterfall Model, Rational Unified Process, Scrum, Kanban and Prototyping. These tools build upon linear thinking. However, reactions to situations in IT projects remain mostly organic. The level of talent and aptitude of the IT project members determines what process or philosophy to use and adapt. Even though some processes are standardized and mandatory in the software life cycle management and also certified as the Capability Maturity Model Integration (CMMI), the execution remains mostly organic.

The task of the ITP coach is to fully engage in the observation of the organic process. The linear process is monitored through established tools.

The magic bullet lies in ITP coach's ability to mindfully respond to the organic talents and creative ideas exhibited and presented by team members. These talents and creative ideas often run counter to linear processes.

Another critical point can be illustrated by a test which you can engage in wherever there is water. Imagine opening a faucet just a little bit. Water droplets fall rhythmically. Open the faucet a little bit more, the water droplets fall a little faster, but still rhythmically. At a certain point of opening the faucet, the water loses the rhythm completely and gushes out—somewhat uncontrollably.

IT projects move along at a steady pace or rhythm but at some point the system shifts into the chaos. There is information overload or not enough information. There are different resolutions to the same problem. Linear thinking no longer works. As IT projects all over the world become more and more complex, we need highly qualified and skilled ITP coaches. IT project coaching as a success story will be readily welcomed in this environment.

Recapitulation of the themes of this chapter:
- Building a success story with the collective learning approach in the ITP coaches network and following tasks of an ITP coach;
- Accompanying IT projects up from the development of the business case;
- Selective meeting participation - within the project team, as well as with stakeholders;
- Coaching sessions with all "key roles" of the project team;
- Field reports on project management and stakeholders;
- Ensuring "Lessons Learned" scenarios;
- Summation and perfecting of all these characteristics.

The support of the coach in the world of information leads then to the whistleblowing topic. The theme of linearity to organic passes through the chaos theory.

4

Underline the Importance of "Human" in Human Capital

Motivation is the road to success

As Cargo ships need a pilot to safely navigate through risky waters, IT projects need a coach. The ship's crew responds to the pilot's directives for successful navigation through risky waters. Similarly project team members—people—respond to the insights of ITP coach.

> *You always make the most money doing what you most enjoy.*
> Mark Twain

Twain's words are appropriate in the business world. We know that success rates for projects increase if the employees are motivated to work their best.

The ITP coaching approach sets humans in the center of action. This attention generates a feeling of respect by the team members which in turns increases their motivation to work and to succeed. And that enhances the sense of enjoyment and accomplishment through work.

Motivation is an important implement that is often under-utilized by managers in today's working environment. They use motivation in the workplace to inspire people to work and to produce the best outcomes for business in the most effective and operational way. Long time traditional thinking holds that motivation has to be generated from the outside. Now we understand that each individual has his own set of motivating forces. Together with the support of the ITP coach, the manager carefully identifies and addresses these motivational powers.

Motivation is key in the ITP coach approach. This chapter discusses motivation in detail. Chapters 5 and 7 also discuss the power of motivation.

Understand through questions

A highly respected mentor once said to me, "If you want to know what constitutes positive, mental health and happiness to a person, then you just have to ask this person." In a one to one coaching session, the ITP coach asks this question of the team members. The answers given leads to a better understanding of requirements, purposes and tasks of the project team. Asking individuals what motivates them and helps them to work their best enhances the ITP coach's ability to gain recognition and trust from the team members.

By asking questions, the ITP coach orchestrates the necessary interactions that result in desired conceptual understanding. Intellectually engaging questions help stimulate and focus IT project members' thinking while helping the ITP coach understand them individually. The information gained and possibilities created by subtle changes in phrasing questions increase the tools an ITP coach can utilize. Team members observe that the ITP coach listens and adapts the project to best utilize the skills of the team members. That results in a fruitful, supportive, constructive and motivating working environment.

If you enjoy your work, you are prepared in a holistic way for your entire life. Professionally satisfied and established people are a powerful success factor. Motivation is not only a business factor it's important for the whole society.

To ask questions is the simplest and most effective way of learning. Children and students learn by asking questions. New employees learn by asking questions and innovators understand clients' need by asking questions. Great leaders know that this is the best way to gain deeper insights.

"What is the one thing I should do to make things better for you," was Greg Dyke's question when he went to every major meeting with the staff, as he became general director of the BBC. He followed this with another question, "What is the one thing I should do to make things better for our viewers and listeners?" Greg knew at that early phase he could learn more from his employees than they could from him. By asking them questions he used a very powerful tool.

Why does the moon not fall into the Earth?
Isaac Newton

All great thinkers and scientists asked and ask questions. For the ITP coach, asking questions is part of the daily business routine. The answers given by team members to the questions are respected and listened to very carefully and dealt respectfully. This builds trust between the ITP manager and the ITP team.

The ITP coach asks open questions in order to give the IT project members a chance to offer their insights.

Examples of open questions are:
• What other possibilities should we consider?
• How can we reduce workload in this project?
• Why do you think this challenge has happened?

As ITP coaches listen carefully to the answers, they formulate further questions. The best approach is to continue asking questions of the team members. In doing so, the ITP coach guides the team in recognizing the comprehensive nature of the project. Once all team members understand the breadth and depth of the project, then collectively they determine a course of action.

That course of action is further defined more questions. This time the ITP coach asks the IT project members closed questions, giving them a limited choice of responses. The coach gets specific information from the team members. This refines the process even more. By continuing this kind of question/discuss, the ITP coach deliberately moves the conversation forward in a particular direction.

ITP Coaching for motivation and performance

In well managed businesses, the managers work to improve business performance through effective motivation of employees while meeting the needs of the organization's employees. Employee well-being is or should be a major concern. A critical element of *The Trillion Dollar IT Revolution* demands giving consideration to how the ITP coaching approach consistently contributes to improving business performance by highly motivated people and excellent teamwork.

People are the organization's key resource. Overall organizational performance largely depends on them. If, therefore, an appropriate range of ITP coaching and processes is developed and implemented effectively, then human motivation makes a substantial impact on solid performance. There is a clear, direct link between ITP coach practices and organizational performance.

The ITP coach is able to check if the project management provides individuals with stimulating and interesting work and gives them the autonomy and flexibility to perform these jobs well. Important goals focus on are:

- Enhance job satisfaction and flexibility, which encourages greater performance and productivity;
- Enlarge the skill base and develop the levels of competence required in the workforce;
- Encourage people to identify themselves with and act upon the core values of the organization and willingly contribute to the achievement of organizational goals;

- Develop a climate of cooperation and trust in the team;
- Establish a performance culture that encourages high performance in such areas as productivity, quality and growth in a motivating and self-evident manner;
- Empower employees to risk taking, innovation and sharing of knowledge, and establishes trust between managers and subordinates;
- Generate motivation, commitment and job engagement by valuing team players in accordance with their contribution.

All these should flow naturally for top management. It is critical to monitor all these points from a neutral position. The approach of the ITP coach is to guarantee that the ITP coach occupies that neutral position.

Coaching definitions

Business coaching is very well established in the professional life. Business coaching is a type of personal or human resource development. It provides positive support, feedback and advice to an individual or in a group basis to improve personal or individual effectiveness in the business setting.

The difference between business coaching and ITP coaching is the network and collective learning approach in a special market niche—the IT projects.

In IT projects, a strong technical focus is related to the system itself. The ITP coach keeps focus on individual team member strengths which then strengthen the overall team power. In the ITP coach approach, the whole team benefits.

A living ITP coach can do things that this book can't, mainly he or she can listen to a person and when the person asks a question or mentions an objection, he or she can respond to it. Obviously, no book is that flexible, so the book's contents have to address all the essential questions and objections. All good project management tactics and theories have good and effective methodologies. The ITP coaches network is a living experience which allows for implementation the latest findings. The key component is to monitor implementation!

We will discuss these advantages in more detail in later chapters.

I'm like a doctor with great medicine to heal the reader's pain; confidently I tell you that and ask you to take the medicine now so you and your company can begin to heal. Act now. Take the medicine of ITP coaching to your IT business.

On www.itpcoach.com/02 you will find the latest news about excellent human motivation and team power.

The founders' motivation return

In the early years of IT, several companies approached the work as more of a hobby and pleasure. Microsoft and Apple were two such examples.

As notable successes accumulated, pressure increased within multinationals to continue the string of successes. Pressure generated stress in the work place. Here it is important to take into account the latest developments and the ITP coaches network symbolizes an ingenious way to do that.

A *New York Times* article on June 16, 2012, says: "To Stay on Schedule, Take a Break"

A growing body of evidence shows that taking regular breaks from mental tasks improves productivity and creativity. Skipping breaks can lead to stress and exhaustion. Mental concentration is similar to a muscle, says John P. Trougakos, an assistant management professor at the University of Toronto-Scarborough and the Rotman School of Management. The brain becomes fatigued after sustained use and needs a rest period before it can recover, he explains. Think of the competitors in weight lifting events. Each athlete needs rest before doing a second round of repetitions at the gym. Breaks can induce guilt because they're some sort of little oasis of personal time that we get while we're selling ourselves to someone else. But that's just the point. Employees generally need to detach from their work and their work space to recharge their internal resources. Options include walking, reading a book in another room or taking the all-important lunch break, which provides both nutritional and cognitive recharging. It's shortsighted not to take this time, or for managers to discourage employees from taking it. Try to take a break before reaching the absolute bottom of your mental barrel.

Most workers don't take enough breaks, and if they do, they often remain seated. Physical movement is necessary in order to gain the most benefit when taking a break according to Professor James A. Levine. Studies done by Professor Levine show that worker who remain sedentary throughout the day impair their health. When it comes to productivity and concentration, everyone has a different capacity. Management should encourage employees to generate individual, effective break routines.

They also encourage those flashes of genius that employers' value so much, adds Levine, noting that Albert Einstein is thought to have conceived the theory of relativity while riding his bicycle.

"For us believing physicists, the demarcation between past, present and future has merely the significance of but a persistent illusion."
Albert Einstein
(from his letter of condolence to Bice and Vero Besso 21.3.1955)

Well-defined and successful targets

Another important point in this context is establishing real values and purpose to setting consistent goals. Einstein had set the goal to be a good physicist, so he was ready to create a superior theory.

Values contribute to our strategy to turn our expertise into powerful goals. In business, good planning and goal setting are essential. In this way, an employee can achieve his best work based upon his own knowledge and understanding. In turn, the employee can generate the income and the recognition that is desired. Our personal purpose and vision propel our business ethics and work. Purpose and vision exist in the core of our being. Purpose and vision are our expressions of our essential being. Our purpose opens our doors to our passion and when we are living our purpose and expressing it out into the world, we are positioned to do an outstanding job.

This deep human aspect of our purpose is the reason we believe we are on earth. This purpose guides us as we seek to make a positive difference in our own and other people's lives. We are passionate about our lives and about our goals and about what we're doing in life. Employees who live in accordance with their purpose excel. They're motivated because they know clearly what is at their core and they are fully expressing it.

A good coaching praxis helps people to find their values and purposes. An ITP coach creates a great win-win situation to be written in the human success stories. Companies with top motivated employees achieve the best results on the market and in the context of values and purpose realize a very sustainable success.

A big secret to setting goals that truly inspire and motivate you is to identify goals that are aligned with your values, your purpose, and the vision of the future that correspond with your profession. This procedure really underlines the meaning of "human" in human capital.

Goal setting is outlined in the next chapter. Effective goal setting becomes an excellent objective because effective goal setting establishes a foundation for significant savings in and compelling use of money, time and human motivation.

Recapitulation of the themes of this chapter:
- Increasing success rates occurs with motivated employees;
- Asking questions leads to a better understanding of the project team;

- Utilizing ITP coaching motivates individuals to work for higher performance;
- Recognizing the difference between business coaching and ITP coaching;
- Realizing the difference between the founding years of IT and the current working pressure and how break times help to increase productivity;
- Establishing values and purpose and monitoring goal setting enhances the likelihood of success.

5

Save Significantly:
Money, Time, and Human Motivation

Enjoy work and multiply success

As mentioned earlier in this book, studies indicate that IT demonstrates a strong need to leverage leadership and communication within the teams. The overall purpose of *The Trillion Dollar IT Revolution* is to establish a unique and sustainable IT coaching approach in order to significantly increase success rates of IT projects while creating an environment that helps people enjoy work. When implemented, the IT coaching approach delivers huge savings in dollar and time while significantly reducing employee burnout in IT Project Management.

Having motivated employees is essential to any business's success. How then can managers in particular motivate workers? Is it possible for individuals to motivate themselves? Let's take a look at the question of motivation.

If the employees and team members are motivated to do their work, the business success rates will be much higher. If the success rates are higher, then IT projects are moving more efficiently. Time is not wasted in dragging and pushing projects that are not going to succeed. Employees are less frustrated. In fact, employees become more motivated because they see what success can bring. Employees can focus on more attractive tasks again. This in turn results in a further increase of the success rates.

The form of motivation has a direct impact on sustainable success. Delegation of tasks is very powerful and can save money and time, by helping to build skills and, in turn, by motivating people. You can read more in chapter 7 on how to generate the delegation of tasks to achieve powerful results.

Motivational awareness

Intrinsic motivation refers to motivation that is driven by an interest or enjoyment in the commitment itself. I use the term commitment in relation to the intrinsic motivation because in my life, I received consistent and insightful feedback from motivated people who enjoyed their work. When such individuals share with others, one recognizes that they speak from a strong commitment to their mission.

In my time as a delegate of the employee representation of a leading Swiss bank, I maintained an active dialogue between employees and management. For example, an employee responsible for dealing in old coins was very motivated to attend auctions of antique coin dealers. For him it was more a hobby than a job. A top management member once shared with me that he viewed his work as more an honor than a task.

Extrinsic motivation refers to the performance of a function in order to attain an outcome, whether or not that activity is also intrinsically motivated. Today, top management appears to engage in extrinsic motivation; at least that is what I hear from the managers of the old guard.

When the media chooses to discuss the high salaries of senior executives, it is often difficult to understand staff reduction. Competition is also an extrinsic motivator because it encourages the performer to win and to beat others, not simply to enjoy the intrinsic rewards of the job. If jobs are disappearing, this kind of competition becomes exceedingly unmotivating if at the same time high salaries of management are in the news. The resulting competitive mode emerges as a huge challenge against team power. When information is withheld and other tactics against their own team members are applied, a dauntingly insurmountable obstacle to project success will be the result. This is probably the number one reason that so many IT projects are unsuccessful.

Especially under these conditions, teamwork makes the motivation work. If highly motivated ITP coaches work with the IT project members on a sustaining success, all involved find enjoyment in the work which increases the motivation to leverage processes and produce high quality outcomes. This relegates useless media reports to the background while bringing focus on the project goals. Successful project members gain job security. Motivated and successful employees can close the gap between wages and salaries and feel more adequately compensated when the next round of wage negotiations occurs.

A number of motivational theories emphasize the distinction between conscious and unconscious motivations. Through simple dialogue in a coaching setting, the real source for motivation will become apparent. The reknown psychologist Sigmund Freud is associated with the idea that human beings have many unconscious motivations derived from unconscious emotions that influence how they make important decisions. It is even more important to make known the emotions which trigger improper or inappropriate misbehavior with colleagues. If an employee feels anxious or uncertain of team member reaction to information, the employee may not share that information even though it would be very important for his colleagues to know. The ITP coach approach brings to awareness the real motivation for individuals and the team. In doing so, the ITP coached team clearly recognizes its objectives and consciously implements them.

On this successful way a lot of time will be saved by avoiding miscommunications and the motivation of the team will be strengthened.

The ITP coaching approach is the simple recipe for this success story.

Center the attention to human being

ITP coaches must possess a keen awareness of the signs of "burn-out." The most motivated employees are often confronted with stress and work overload. This can lead to employee burn-out. ITP coaches must be alert to signs of burn-out within team members and do all they can to prevent it from happening. Burn-out rates are high among "lone rangers." IT specialists are often lone rangers because there are few people like them in their immediate environment. ITP coaches will emphasize working together and taking a team approach on all matters inherent to a project. ITP coaches closely monitor the actions and work ethic of the team members. If they see signs of burn-out, they address it immediately. Otherwise the risk is great that the project may lose a good specialist.

In my business career, I have had a formative experience that I want to share with you. A decade ago I worked as an IT project manager in the Swiss banking business. In addition, I worked as a delegate to the employee representatives. As an employee representative, I felt as if I were a lone fighter against injustice. This feeling of being alone intensified when my father died and shortly afterwards one of my colleagues died in an accident. I took over the duties of my work colleague. That added to my burden. The death of two people who were close to me brought me to my limits. I wanted to talk about it with anyone. I believed that talking would provide proof of my strength and ability to work clear headed. I became more and more stressed.

During this time, a coach would have been worth gold for me. I believe that all who are involved in IT projects have a natural tendency to take on too much and, work as a lone ranger. In the coaching session the challenges that lead to being a lone ranger are visible and the team can react accordingly.

The most important point is to act now. Begin now to create this ITP coaches network and to participate in this success story.

The average company lists "at-risk projects" for several million dollars every year. This risk level can be reduced and money saved while workers grow in their sense of accomplishment when companies implement the ITP coaching approach.

The important trust factor

We know that it takes time to build trust. Even more time can be needed to overcome long standing, bad conditions or processes that have destroyed employee confidence and morale. This troubling situation exists because, as noted several times, about half of all IT projects fail. Companies have to overcome this poor history. It is very important to act now, to fix processes that have not worked so that employee confidence and morale can begin to grow.

Finally all this results in the fact that an IT company can save a lot of money and time. Successful projects also preserve human motivation. This reinforces trust in all IT areas.

The great advantage of this success story is that participating companies can save a lot of money in their implementation. This emerges from all the reliable people who come together from the participating companies to form an amazing ITP coaches network. An ITP coach generates added value for various projects.

Please read more about this in chapter 9—how interested companies send their reliable people and how they form their own network. Chapter 10 (first subchapter: Trust is basic) also underlines the importance of trust from and to the management as well as from and to the employees.

The latest news about this truly holistic approach can be found at www.itpcoach.com/03.

The effective Pareto principal

Monitoring the 80-20 rule, also known as the Pareto's Principle, supports the ITP coach in being more effective in IT projects. Pareto's Principle helps manage those things that really make a difference in the results of the IT project.

In 1906, Vilfredo Pareto observed that 80 percent of the land in Italy was owned by 20 percent of the population. Pareto also noted that 20 percent of the pea pods in his garden contained 80 percent of the peas. Between 1930 and 1940 the Quality Management pioneer, Dr. Joseph Juran, drew upon Pareto's observations and documented a universal principle he called the "vital few and trivial many" and reduced it to writing. Juran called it the Pareto Principle. The principle states that 20 percent of something is always responsible for 80 percent of the results. In some companies 20 percent of the staff will provide 80 percent of the production. Project Managers know that the first 10 percent and the last 10 percent of the work consume 80 percent of time and resources.

The value of the 80-20 rule for a manager is that it reminds the manager to focus on the 20 percent that matters. By identifying and focusing on those things that matter, the 20 percent produce 80 percent of the results. The objective then is to monitor employees so that they are not devoting 80 percent of their work time to reach the last 20 percent of the result. Supporting the good to become better is a more efficient use of time than in assisting the great to become terrific. That the Pareto Principle is used wisely can be perfectly monitored by an ITP coach.

The same also applies with the "90–9–1 principle" which states that in a collaborative website such as a Wikipedia, 90% of the participants of a community only view content, 9% of the participants edit content, and 1% of the participants actively create new content. If we apply this 90–9–1 principle to an internet community, we can argue that 1% of the users of a website actively create new content, while the other 99% of the participants only lurk. A lurker is typically a member of an online community who observes, but does not actively participate. For example, for every person who posts on a forum, generally about 99 other people are only passively consuming that content.

Both can be compared with the Pareto principle that 20 percent of a group will produce 80 percent of the activity, regardless of how the activity may be defined.

The actual percentage of the internet using rules most likely varies depending upon the subject matter. For example, if a forum requires content submissions as a condition of entry, the percentage of people who participate will probably be significantly higher, but the content producers will still remain a minority of users.

If you coach a person, then the person subconsciously knows the best way to improve a situation. Often only a small percentage of the IT project team is actively involved in the improvement. The ITP coach can optimally support the passive percentage of the team to activate their strengths, their talent. Thus, untapped potential can be actively exploited.

An old saying goes: "if it sounds too good to be true, it probably is" but the ITP coach approach has so many tools to draw upon that the approach can and does work.

ITP coaching improves project management

To clearly illustrate why a coach can save a lot of money and time, while turning around employees' loss of motivation, I would like to address some aspects of project management.

Good project management is based upon clear rules. Good coaching helps to make these guidelines known to the project team and supports the team to maintain compliance with the guidelines.

Important parts of project management to be monitored by an ITP coach are:

1. Project Planning

Financial planning (expenses / costs / benefits), work breakdown structure, settlement plan with clearly defined objectives, schedules, resource plan, organization chart, information and documentation plan with clear scheduling—these are all major issues in project planning. Their successful execution is the goal of successful project management. The ITP coach supervises the implementation of the processes to attain these items.

2. Project Marketing

When the stakeholder management is used properly, the communication between the stakeholder and the IT project team supports the project success. The ITP coach maintains awareness of the communication needs in a project. This enables risk minimization thus increasing the likelihood of success and appropriate project marketing.

3. Change Management

Change orders can and frequently do occur while an IT project is in process. Effective change management demands being able to determine the source of the change order and why the change (or amendment) is necessary. Identifying the sources or sources is critical for proper cost accounting.

How are problems and changes communicated within the team? How are these issues received or perceived? Does change management affect the project objectives? If so, how, why and where does that impact the process? The ITP coach, as a neutral person concerned with the ultimate success of the project, considers the issues and provides the necessary answers. The ITP coach can then adjust the process as needed to maintain the goals and objectives established in the project planning phase. The ITP coach addresses both IT and business concerns.

4. Risk Management

Risk management is commonly viewed differently on management, project portfolio and project management levels. These differences can be neutralized by the ITP coach. The project manager applies the risk analysis during the identification, analysis and evaluation process and initiates appropriate action. What risks actually materialized during the project? What anticipated risks never did occur? This information should be analyzed with the results included in the project follow up. Through the support of the ITP coach, the measures taken are documented and incorporated into a lesson learned.

5. Team Management

A highly functioning project team builds upon a foundation of motivation, communication, structure and trust. The professional competence should be balanced with other skills, to acquire the methods applied and the structures of the team foundation.

The human factor plays a critical role in the success of any project. The ITP coach must have strong skill sets in working with the human factor. This topic is addressed in detail in chapter 7.

6. Project Management Office (PMO) and Project Controlling: Depending on the size of the project supported by PMO and applied by project controlling, there are important control processes. For IT projects, pressure arises from project management to the PMO to do the entire project assistance workload. Project controlling means that the project will be monitored in a defined time interval. This generates pressure on the project management. The coach can work to connect these points and prevent pressure.

In a continuous process, all issues are monitored by the ITP coach:
- What progress has been achieved so far and what has not;
- Have the deliverables attained the intended levels required so far;
- Did goals and no-goals really get what the stakeholder wanted;
- Did the project get the quality level of results that were anticipated?

The continuous process supports the project management in being prepared for any necessary tweaking; it also removes the pressure of management to place undue pressure on the PMO.

7. Goal Management

Objectives are clearly defined from the start of a project. While a project is in process, it is important to check whether system-scope and stakeholder-scope match. Sometimes factors such as cost and time affect and influence specs in the project. Changes occur. Therefore, during the execution of a project, it is important to establish a clear distinction between targets and change management.

The ITP coach makes all this obvious through ongoing coaching sessions with the project members. These sessions provide the channel through which changing information and their impact on the project is shared and discussed.

By keeping the acronym SMART in mind, one has a much higher probability of reaching the goals of the project. The ITP coach supports the whole project team in this approach.

A SMART goal is:
- Specific—you know exactly what you want to accomplish;
- Measurable—you can measure whether or not you are making progress to reach it;
- Achievable and attainable—you know that you can realistically achieve it;
- Relevant—pertinent to the project and the process. The ITP coach checks periodically to determine that the goals remain relevant;
- Time-based—a specific time by which a goal will be accomplished. The ITP coach supports the team to aim for attainable times.

Another interpretation to SMART is:
- Sensitive;
- Mindful;
- Attentive;
- Respectful;
- Tolerant.

These are also excellent skills for an ITP coach.

In a study in 1979, Harvard graduates were asked if they had clear written goals including plans on how to achieve the goals. Less than 5 % did. Another 10 % had goals but not in writing. The rest had no specific goals at all. The authors of the study interviewed the graduates ten years later. The researchers discovered that the former students who had had goals but had not put them in writing were earning twice as much as the rest that had no goals at all. The big discovery was that the students who had clearly written goals when they left the university were earning, on average, 10 times as more than all the others of their classmates combined.

In a similar fashion, the ITP coach works to obtain feedback: Are project goals actually written and are the goals are clearly understood. When goals are written and understood, the team has a greater sense of security. Along with that security comes a greater willingness to be flexible when tackling the process. Most important, teams demonstrate greater resilience when they encounter any unexpected obstacles.

Chapter 8 (subchapters 3 and 4) also underline the importance of clear targets.

Effective and successful project management involves many other important areas. Here I have addressed those which I believe are the most important.

Please go to www.itpcoach.com/04 for additional information on what an ITP coach brings to project management. You will also see how an ITP coach can help project teams save significant amounts of money and time while sustaining the human motivation element.

Summary of the themes of this chapter:

- Multiply success rates of IT projects to enable people to enjoy their work;
- Improve motivation by making it conscious;
- Counter the Burn-Out challenge successfully with human scope;

- Build trust to close an important gap in IT project management;
- Monitor the 80-20 rule to be more effective in IT projects;
- Improve overall project management by using an ITP coach who knows the right tools to use to save time and money and to increase employee motivation.

Actual Challenges in IT Project Management

Challenging global and local factors

We live in a time in which both global issues and local factors affect IT projects. The challenges we face cannot be remedied with the same level of thinking and solutions that have worked in the past.

Cloud computing is one of many examples. The popularity of the term can be attributed to its use in marketing hosted services that run client server software from a remote location. With cloud computing, emotional security issues emerge that center on concern for confidential business data. New processes demand new ways of thinking. The collective learning approach of the ITP coaches network provides the arena for such new ways of thinking and approaching problem resolution.

Specifically, interdisciplinary communication challenges accentuate themselves in the global labor market. The work force found in multinational corporations brings together people from diverse cultures and language.

This point brings me back to the analogy of the pilot for big ships. An experienced captain trusts in the wisdom and experience of a local pilot to navigate the ship around hazards. Similarly, an experienced ITP coach informs the project team of hazards and risks in an IT project.

More than half of the respondents to a monthly McKinsey labor review (November 2006 global survey) expect intensifying competition for talent—and the increasingly global nature of that competition—to have a major effect on their companies over the next several years. Unfortunately millions of people on a global labor market do not always mean the skills, experience and education that your company requires are readily available. With an increase in candidates applying for each open position, recruiting actually gets harder, not easier. The ability to have good working pools and to find the specialist you so desire presents the real challenge. You find more about the pool approach and the incomparable advantage of the ITP coach framework in chapter 10.

How the employees express their challenges

The project team is often so deeply rooted in the daily operations and under significant time constraints that they fail to notice hazards and risks. The ITP coach's perspective brings these significant problem areas into view. The ITP coach can then work with the project team to address and overcome the hazards, risks and challenges. The fluctuation of top IT specialists is a big challenge for IT companies. There are various reasons for a change, but some of them can be clearly avoided in a personal dialogue. The "inner dialogues" people often engage in can lead to strange results. In a coaching conversation, such internal dialogue can be discussed and analyzed. This leads to an exploration of possible challenges. A challenge facing each highly excellent IT specialist is recognizing his tendency to see only his program, his source code, his area of expertise and not recognize other issues, paths or solutions as the specialist dives very deeply into their matter.

We don't see things as they are, we see them as we are.
Anaïs Nin

People from different cultures have different ways to express or not express important thoughts. An experienced ITP coach with solid training in understanding cultural differences combined with many years of project experience brings a significant advantage to project management, just as does the pilot who knows the local navigable waterway well.

In most regions and especially in all major ports, using a harbor pilot is a legal obligation. A container ship that attempts to save the cost of an experienced pilot risks incurring immense costs from damages incurred in navigating unfamiliar waters. This argument could apply in a general meeting of shareholders that the company adopt a statutory requirement for using an ITP coach.

It is critical that managers understand how helpful and motivating an ITP coach can be. When potential problems are identified early on and eliminated because of the insights of an ITP coach, project members become even more motivated and dedicated to achieving a successful project completion. The team knows that the ITP coach's insight keeps them from wasting time and energy. Early resolution or even complete elimination of problems not only enhances the likelihood of profitability in the project, but also generates a better and more targeted implementation of the IT project. The ITP coach communicates the concerns of the involved stakeholders in a direct and neutral form to the project team. All of this results in a better user implemented and applicable final solution.

Thomas Edison is noted for his comment on the invention of the light bulb, "I have not failed. I've just found 10,000 ways that won't work." Companies engaged in IT projects must act now so that Edison's comment does not become a sad commentary as IT people never end their projects successfully. We have to act and to express ourselves in clear and intelligible ways to make accessible to all peoples the true content of projects as reported in our words.

From my position, we now know thousands of ways that IT projects won't work.

It's time now to transform this behavior with the ITP coach approach and to make every IT project a success! Then a powerful success story can illuminate the world!

Be the change that you wish to see in the world.
Mahatma Gandhi

Changes and cost pressure

Staying within budget on any IT project is probably the biggest challenge. As projects proceed, unexpected but logical changes or variations occur in the IT project environment. Variations come with unbudgeted costs. The additional costs trigger added pressure to the project team. Will the project come in on time and on budget? The project environment becomes negatively charged. Worker motivation can plummet. It becomes difficult to recognize what is happening. Senior managers in such a situation struggle to assess the impact the unexpected has on a project team. Moreover, the managers are usually involved in other tasks and have limited time to devote to assessing problems.

In an effort to keep projects on time and on budget, the project manager pressures the team to stay on track. The added pressure undermines the collegial relationship between the project manager and the project team. Adding to the pressure is the continually changing environment in the labor market which results in multi-cultural teams. In an ideal environment, project managers and teams would take time to adapt to these changes, but cost constraints combined with scheduling issues do not allow for it. So the challenges grow steadily. Team members default to ways they have used in the past to handle the unanticipated or unexpected. There is no relief in sight and pressure continues to mount.

In addition, core competencies are weakened by the changing work environment. Domestic specialists are too expensive compared to foreign competition. Practical know-how may be only marginally replaced by theoretical knowledge.

Challenges of the global market

The global labor market does offer a better educated workforce for a lower salary. These highly trained and educated cheap labor forces learn and adapt quickly in foreign environments. They realize their value and leave the jobs for which they were hired to go to a new or even similar job but at a higher wage. Eventually, though, problems will arise.

Let's go back again to the analogy of the pilot. A Philippine crew on a European container ship can do a great job on the high seas. When the crew must navigate a European harbor, the legislature has decided that a local pilot is required. This pilot brings additional and unique skill to the crew: his knowledge of the characteristics of the local waterways.

From the perspective of project staff, severance payments to top executives are quite often seen as arbitrary. Management decisions that impact IT projects also appear arbitrary to the project team. Cultural differences can be the source of the disgruntlement. Another source could be haphazard flow of information on management decisions. The point comes down to the IT project team being adrift. To set the team back on course and to pilot the team through the troubled waters, the ITP coach engages in coaching sessions with the project members. Through these coaching sessions the ITP coach can discover if there are concerns about wage inequality or any other issue.

When parts of an IT project team are left to the decide how to deal with the project developments, disharmony or even frustration can emerge and the team may very well be unaware of it. In a coaching conversation, the ITP coach can identify important clues that result in the disharmony. The ITP coach can name them and determine how to respond to the issues before they become insurmountable. An ITP coach brings to every project the skills, training and insights to address all the emerging issues and changes during the course of the project. The ITP coach's responses keeps employee motivation at a high level which is critical in keeping IT costs from escalating. The work of an IT coach provides a "win-win" environment for employees and employer.

Abuse of power and forced success

Consider migration projects in large companies. If the entire IT infrastructure is to migrate to a new version (Win7 to Win 8), various projects inadvertently jockey for attention on a program level. On the program level one project takes care of the hardware, another focuses on the GUI, another deals with the software, and there are always the interfaces. At the same time there can be up to ten active, independent, large-scale projects, each of which can have quite different management structures. Each of the projects receives a common, overall management process. However, an intense competitive mode prevails among the project managers. When project managers face so many project choices, instead of considering what project could best benefit from their individual leadership/management, managers focus more on their career track and seek to position themselves most favorably within the projects. Power grabs and posturing increase. Each project director works to bring in his project first, fastest and with the best results. Returning to our ships in the harbor comparison, if several large ships entered the same port at the same time, captains could scramble to get the best position to get the best pilot. The scrambling and posturing could generate a highly dangerous situation. Pilots working together can specify a clear and sensible priority in consultation with the appropriate port authority and monitor its implementation. ITP coaches are the harbor pilots who can bring clarity and sensibility to a highly charged changing situation.

Big programs and their communication challenges

In a large bank, I observed the development of a program to migrate the infrastructure to Windows 7. In the first year, virtually no communication occurred among certain projects. Then a manager noticed this lack of communication. He created a task force designed to share information and experiences that would be relevant to each project as Windows 7 was implemented. Unfortunately each project was mired in the muck of uncertainty on how to implement their part in the program. Moreover projects were in differing stages of completion. A merger of involved projects at the program level was no longer feasible.

With an ITP coach assigned to each project, obstructive factors and barriers can be detected and corrected as early as possible.

Destructive competition in innovation

Innovation is an important competitive element. Blind innovation—engaging in innovation for the sake of being innovative—can lead to everything being replaced. Given the different experience level of employees regarding company policies and procedures, understanding of and comfortability with new technologies, project completion times can vary widely. This does not bode well for the company.

We like to believe in business that competition is healthy. It is. However, competition that arises within a company and among its project teams can be costly. It is critical to pay attention to where competition among projects persists and even where struggles to position oneself (career, recognition, advancement, etc.) have already generated into conflict.

Just as a pilot plans together with the port team so that the incoming ships do not interfere with each other, an ITP coach guarantees in a clear, constructive and fair process, an optimal and efficient support of all projects.

Inherent challenges to the system

The term "inherent to the system" refers to a condition that arises from the rules or processes of a system without being explicitly wanted and certainly not desired. The random conditions are not necessarily helpful or beneficial.

A very common example of this is the garden. Anyone who has ever worked in a garden is faced with weeds, although this is not at all intended. The original goal was to make beautiful flowers and other plants thrive. Nevertheless, weeds always come back because weeds are inherent to the garden system.

Many factors which adversely affect an IT project are inherent in the system. An ITP coach will not only identify these challenges but also minimize the negative impact of these factors.

An unconscious incompetency that is inherent to the system can be transformed to a conscious incompetency and subsequently to a conscious competency and strength when an ITP coach is involved in the project.

Society as a system is based on rules. In such a complex system as a society (individuals, state, multinationals), it becomes increasingly impossible to be aware of all the rules and to monitor them. Thus, it is inherent in the system that certain rules are broken. Even if the breaking of rules is unintentional, rule breaking will inevitably happen. Occasions will emerge in which a rule is forgotten or cannot be defined or even remembered. Problems then appear.

An example of this is the ethical code. When the term ethics is discussed in a group of people there will probably be very different understandings of acceptable action or behavior pertinent to a project. All social systems recognize the importance of maintaining loyalty to certain ethics. It is the interpretation and implementation of them out of which challenges emerge.

The job of an ITP coach is to always hold to the observer role. The ITP coach can explain to project team members how their individual understandings of appropriate actions and behavior create problems for the process and what corrective actions need to be taken. A coach must be intentional in his monitoring role. It is his responsibility to maintain vigil over all aspects of the process and keep projects on track.

Systems are subject to inherent complexity. Clients seldom know how, if or when their concerns will be implemented in an IT project. The computer in turn does not know exactly how the client works and what the client expects from the IT system. The ITP coach brings together business representatives, business analysts, IT project managers, developers and many others involved in an IT project to make sure of a solution-oriented implementation.

There are many communication layers involved in a system and so it's inherent that not just one single person cause problems. The role of an ITP coach includes watching these challenges and to make early warning of vulnerabilities.

As an inherent system, delegation is very powerful and can save money and time, by helping to build skills and motivating people. Unfortunately, poor delegation might cause frustration and confusion to all the involved parties. This chapter concludes with this warning, and in the next chapter, the positive power of delegation is emphasized.

Summarization of the themes of this chapter:
- Global and local factors that affect the labor market, methods and goals;
- Challenges that arise because project members have different ways to express themselves;
- Cost pressures in a rapidly changing environment;
- Global labor market exploitation for self-interest;
- Power and success factors that lead to current challenges;
- Communication issues in big programs;
- Projects involving innovative and competitive modes;
- Challenges arise because of matters inherent to the system.

7

The Power of the Team

Delegate to the team power

A critical component for advancing one's career is the ability to establish a team that works well together. Having absolute trust among team members is essential in building a strong team. When trust exists, then project managers can delegate more to the team members.

This then leads to a faster and more efficient implementation of the project.

Delegation occurs when people ask others to perform tasks on their behalf. Delegating responsibilities is very beneficial because we can use it to overcome personal limitations. Each of us has limited time, energy, and talents and this makes the benefit of delegation so important. Delegation increases the project output, when the people to whom the management delegates devote their time, energy and talents to the needs of the IT project. But delegation is also the partnership of authority and responsibility to another person, and this is highly motivating to a subordinate. It is one of the core concepts of management leadership.

I believe that there is a natural affinity between the Stakeholder Centered Coaching by Marshall Goldsmith which offers a leadership coaching approach and the ITP coach approach as discussed in this book. Together they provide a very powerful support process to monitor the positive effects of delegation. Executive coaching is a top down approach to attain high quality, effective delegation. ITP coaching is a bottom up approach to attain high quality, effective delegation.

> *Don't walk behind me; I may not lead. Don't walk in front of me;*
> *I may not follow. Just walk beside me and be my friend.*
> Albert Camus

As a shift of decision-making authority, delegation empowers a subordinate to make decisions. However the person who delegated the work remains accountable for the outcome of the delegated tasks. Delegation is very powerful and can save money and time, by helping to build skills and motivating people. An ITP coach possesses the training and wisdom to effectively monitor, support and balance these factors.

Awareness of the team power

In addition to trust, other characteristics of a strong team include:
- Sharing responsibilities;
- Drawing upon best practices experiences to avoid potential errors;
- Supporting weaker team players;
- Identifying with the project and the target instead of focusing upon one's own future;
- Encouraging freedom of expression and collegial openness to enhance the process;
- Tapping into a wealth of ideas generated by team members;
- Exchanging and rethinking ideas;
- Encouraging and supporting the ideas and efforts of others;
- Offering ideas and reporting their findings to each other;
- Interacting, discussing, and posing questions to all members of the team;
- Offering assistance to each other;
- Practicing mutual support based on trust.

An ITP coach ensures that these characteristics are practiced throughout the life of the project. When these things are practiced, if any type of discord or disagreement arises, it is recognized more quickly. The ITP coach works with the team to eliminate the problems, thus returning the team to its strengths.

ITP coach team power

The old saying that teamwork makes the dream work still holds the highest truth. When team players listen to each other's ideas, motivation and creativity flourish. Each team member willingly contributes to the project. Individual and team motivation remain high. That feeds job satisfaction and the rate of successful projects increases. The ITP coach strengthens the team's cohesiveness by:

- Helping to define individual team members' roles as part of a team;
- Applying teamwork to a range of situations;
- Identifying the strengths of team members;
- Coaching, mentoring and giving feedback;
- Promoting the capacity to communicate effectively with others orally and in writing;
- Advocating interaction and collaboration with others effectively, including in teams, in the workplace, and in culturally or multilingual diverse contexts;
- Encouraging team members to find, evaluate and use information;
- Utilizing discipline, professional skills and knowledge in the workplace;
- Urging team members to rely upon knowledge and skills to devise solutions to unfamiliar problems;
- Providing information regarding research methodologies used in different disciplines as an alternate way to interpret findings;
- Affirming the value of further learning and professional development;

- Applying knowledge derived from numerous disciplines to solve real life problems in communities;
- Emphasizing the importance of professional and personal ethical awareness and academic integrity;
- Accentuating the demand for ethical behavior and social responsibility with regard to social and civic involvement, human rights and sustainability;
- Creating a safe environment where employees from all backgrounds and cultures can make valuable contributions without feeling threatened or vulnerable;
- Developing a climate that values learning in which self-managed learning as well as coaching, mentoring and training flourish.

All these skills are causally significant in today's globalized workplace. Team work that maximizes successful outcomes while continually strengthening the team encourages meaningful interaction with people of different ages, gender, race, religion or political persuasion and optimizes all knowledge learned from those interactions.

Teamwork skills consist of a mix of interactive, interpersonal, problem solving and communication skills which are used by a group of people working together on a common task. Teamwork demands that team members work in complementary roles toward common goals whose outcomes are greater than those possible by any one person working independently.

Motivating team power

The ITP Coach Association trains and sanctions each ITP coach in the knowledge and use of teamwork skills. Having a positive experience as part of a team motivates individual team members. Greater individual motivation results from working with other team members toward a team goal or goals. The greater motivation in turn leads to a greater value being placed on the IT project achievement by the individual, which then results in greater project performance.

Group goals and team member commitment to the goals enhance the likelihood of a team achieving success. The depth of individual and team commitment can be identified, named, measured and guaranteed in the coaching sessions.

Core interactive attributes are communication, teamwork and strong, interpersonal skills. These attributes are necessary in order to engage formally and informally, with a wide range of people and other team players, both internal and external to the organization.

Promoting skills to the team power

An ITP coach constantly promotes the ability to:

- Relate to, and feel comfortable with, people at all levels in the organization as well as to a range of external stakeholders;
- Work effectively in teams, often more than one team at once;
- Make and maintain relationships as circumstances change;
- Adjust roles from one project situation to another in an ever-shifting work situation.

The ability to adjust roles is discussed in detail in the next chapter. Through the ITP Coach Association, members work together to identify other qualities that make a team good and strengthens team performance. Turn to www.itpcoach.com/05 to stay informed.

In a good ITP coaching practice, the team building process is continually monitored. Individual team member's specific responsibilities are predetermined by exacting criteria. Team member effectiveness and contribution level is assessed using evidence from notes and direct observation.

Incorporate the team power

Suggestions on ways to assess teamwork contribution to the project management can include:

- Determining if the team members make clear decisions; who does what in the team and who is responsible for which output;
- Constructing a set of responsibilities and roles in conjunction with the team members to ensure commitment and ownership;
- Providing guidelines on team management and processes and making sure all team players understand them;
- Using teamwork activities when it's essential to achieve the project outcomes and not overusing them;
- Considering appropriate cultural and gender balances in the team;
- Establishing a balance between assessing the team process and product;
- Supporting the process of constructing and managing teams.

Managers have to encourage group work. As the saying goes: groups sink or swim together!

The ITP coach checks individual motivation from a neutral position which significantly increases the probability that the team building process will be accepted by all team members.

Summarization of the themes of this chapter:
- Team building by delegating more and controlling less;
- Strengthening a team and moving the team to live consciously;
- Positive qualities the ITP coach reinforces;
- The motivation of being part of a team and goal commitment;
- Skills that are constantly promoted in the ITP coach approach;
- Suggestions for assessing teamwork to the project management.

8

Actual Challenges versus the Team Power

Approaching an agile solution

All past, current and future challenges leave an impact on the Team. Therefore, it is essential to have a well-designed system that triggers confidence in attacking the challenges and delivering a positive outcome.

The ITP coach approach is that system.

Through the own network, the ITP coach has learned how and is certified to address challenges in a creative and constructive fashion. The ITP coach possesses the requisite tools that he teaches to the project team. The coach begins by demonstrating to the team the advantage experienced in taking on project goals. With a creative and constructive attitude combined with an open and accepting presence, the ITP coach creates a solidly integrated team that does work together. This great attitude will be reflected in the coached IT project team.

This system guides ITP coaches and their teams to attain success and stand as examples to encourage other teams to become winning teams.

The vast body of literature on flexibility does not adequately address the kind of accomplished abilities a company needs to meet its strategic objectives, nor how this flexibility can be achieved. The flexible and agile ITP coaching approach is supported by a versatile network all around the world. The challenge in a globalized world is to transform teams into agile and accomplished teams of worldwide specialists.

Coaching a team to become agile and accomplished typically ranges from several weeks to several months, depending on the IT project. Its principle purpose is to enable team practitioners to develop the skills and working knowledge they need to adapt efficient practices autonomously and effectively within their work environment. This coaching focuses especially on communication, knowledge and ability. There are a lot of other coaching approaches to combine in a flexible manner to reach a successful solution.

The ethos of the ITP coaches network is to extend and use technology to enable extremely rapid delivery of business intelligence and communication solutions. These capabilities are a direct response to the agile system in today's IT world. The concept is aimed at helping the clients build a masterful IT project structure to drive keen information management wrapped up in a powerful delivery of IT solutions. Through the use of enterprising, information-management-focused and experienced coaches, the ITP coach approach can deliver action oriented and measureable results at a velocity that will help transform your business.

The core idea of the ITP coaches network leads directly to an adequate response on current challenges. In chapters 9 and 10 you will read about the importance of a strong ITP coaches network. Additionally, you will find on www.itpcoach.com/06 news about this core network idea.

Team power by collective learning

According to collective learning theory, being part of a strong and successful team provides additional motivation for the individual team members. When the team achieves its goals, then the team as a whole and the team members as individuals want to maintain momentum. They want to continue the success. This high degree of motivation combined with the collective learning approach transforms the current challenges into a means to display and enhance excellent team power.

Most employers value teamwork skills in their profession as highly, if not more highly, than the ability to work independently. Especially in the actual challenges of a globalized workplace is teamwork in great demand. In the workplace, employers are often assigned to project teams over whose pool organization or task focus they have no control. They need to be adaptable and flexible. They have to be able to interact easily with other people while keeping the team's goals as the number one priority.

Ease of ability to work in a cross-disciplinary, cross cultural team is a highly coveted workplace attribute for global players. Many employers consider the ability to work in teams as absolutely critical. The ITP coach approach supports the establishment and continuation of team power skills.

The highest power of these teamwork skills emerges from the sourcing that occurs because of the combination of ideas and solutions available with the collective learning approach. All individual learning experiences will be multiplied in the collective. The global workplace has some challenges but the greatest advantage is that extraordinary people from all over the world are able to learn from each other and grow in vision in a collective learning team.

Collective learning is fundamentally a type of learning that happens in various industries. IBM first introduced *InnovationJams* in 2006 by inviting employees from different countries to join in a massive, open brainstorming session. Large companies like Amazon, Boeing, IBM, P&G and Merck have been crowdsourcing ideas to foster innovation. The people involved in the actively shared ideas are collaboratively developing new knowledge. In the innovation jam they learn through the knowledge sharing and knowledge creation processes. Another example of an innovation jam is *Cisco i-zone*, where people openly share ideas that could be converted into new approaches or solutions or products. Thousands of people contributed to hundreds of ideas in this adventure.

Companies' employees are using intranet tools to share their wisdom across the broader workplace environment to get collaborative projects up and running quickly. There are also many databases in the internet to share knowledge.

The challenge of how to encourage experts to contribute their knowledge is dissolved in the collective learning approach. Encouraging people to share their knowledge openly is important for collective learning. Many studies indicate that people who contribute their knowledge to a global network became the recognized experts over time, as a reason of their visibility and willingness to share.

Collective learning takes place by people who are working on a similar goal and are collaboratively building knowledge and additional skills. Collective learning is the way of bridging the gap between formal education and a modern, agile and challenging IT industry.

Dissolve challenges in the procurement process

For a company, an intelligent management of the IT hardware assets is critical to ensure that IT delivers business value.

Managing software assets is vital for maintaining a highly flexible and market conforming IT platform. The challenge is that often software is purchased by the IT department out of necessity and then forgotten due to its intangible form.

To evolve software asset management tools into complex systems and to use them correctly can help to maintain the company's software purchases. This in turn helps to better meet business needs while remaining compliant with their software contracts. These challenging matters can be perfectly monitored by the ITP coach. It is a perfect example of the team power of their network.

The neutral role of the ITP coach is crucial. The power of their network which provides access to all the ITP coaches' collective experience delivers an excellent overview about successful steps in hardware and software management. In their network, the ITP coaches practice powerful teamwork and stay informed with a collective knowledge about the latest trends. This knowledge base supports monitoring correct and goal-oriented processes in the coaching with IT project members.

In hardware and software management, the first step is to carry out a full asset discovery. The majority of systems management tools will be able to support this task, but the capabilities of the systems may not provide exactly what is needed or may not be sufficient. At this point the feedback from the staff base through the ITP coach is essential.

If a malfunction or an incorrect process is detected, it can be solved successfully. For this reason, multinationals systematically deal with these risks through risk management to consciously recognize risks in a controlled manner and to take advantage of any opportunities that arise. Take the team power of the ITP coaches network now to support your risk management.

Sustainable target definitions

In his book *The 8th Habit*, Dr. Stephen R. Covey writes of a poll of 23,000 employees drawn from a number of companies and industries.

Of those who replied, the poll results indicate:

- Only 37 percent said they have a clear understanding of what their organization is trying to achieve and why;
- Only one in five was enthusiastic about their team's and their organization's goals;
- Only one in five said they had a clear "line of sight" between their tasks and their team's and organization's goals;
- Only 15 percent felt that their organization fully enables them to execute key goals;
- Only 20 percent fully trusted the organization they work for.

Then, Covey superimposes a very human metaphor over the statistics. He says:

If, say, a soccer team had these same scores, only 4 of the 11 players on the field would know which goal is theirs. Only 2 of the 11 would care. Only 2 of the 11 would know what position they play and know exactly what they are supposed to do. And all but 2 players would, in some way, be competing against their own team members rather than the opponent.

Chip Heath, *Made to Stick: Why Some Ideas Survive and Others Die*

The challenges to set sustainable target definitions that are understood by the entire staff are huge. Establishing measurable and recognizable goals increases the probability of success for a good and strong team. With SMART goals, an ITP coach easily monitors progress and provides clear feedback as the team pursues the successful completion of the project. A success story is "born."

Sustainable target definition requires participation of qualified people in its planning and execution. It must involve, respond to, and be accountable to the people who will live with the results of the goals. The target definitions must be economically effective and economic analysis must take into account some critical external factors. Environmental impacts, on the other hand, are those that affect employees directly and over different timeframes. In chapter 6 are mentioned different challenges which serve to make conscious these critical factors. The team power of the ITP coaches network supports the ability to be aware of the challenging factors and to transform them in successful formulation of reachable goals.

The ITP coach approach generates important feedback to leaders so that they adjust their target definitions and this increases the probability that targets are successfully set, understood and implemented.

Actual worksite success stories can be found at www.itpcoach. com/07.

Clear target communication

Another important aspect about setting goals, communicating and understanding them is reflected in the analogy of the rope pulling. In the past millennium, it was easy to practice the sport of rope drag, also known as tug of war. This is a sport that directly pits two teams against each other in a test of strength. In the following picture two teams comprised of four members each tug against each other:

Illustration 6: rope drag, also known as tug of war

In the complexity of today's IT technologies and the complexity of management structures, objectives are more ambiguous than ever. They may even be incomprehensible. Let's consider again the analogy of rope pulling. The following illustration demonstrates the ambiguity spoken of in Covey's poll:

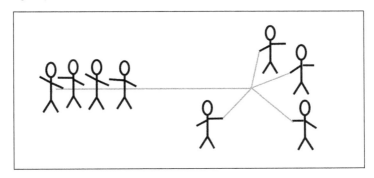

Illustration 7: pull in different directions

If the goals are not fully understood nor addressed properly in a team, the team players, though grouped together on one side, will pull in different directions. Success is greatly compromised, maybe even made impossible to attain.

Which illustration do you want for your teams, your company? I believe most companies function as the team on the right in illustration 7. Consistent success can only occur when teams are aligned as in illustration 6.

Visualize when other firms in your business are adapting the ITP coaching approach, but in your company the teams are pulling in different directions—this result in a strong competitive disadvantage for your company.

Imagine if other firms in your business elect to use the ITP coaching approach, while your company continues with status quo. Your company will be at a serious disadvantage and that does not bode well for gross income and profits. Imagine though, if you become first in your industry to learn and implement the ITP coaching system. Now who has the advantage? Isn't that what you want?

Clear, target communication demands that each team member knows exactly his place and his tasks. In multinationals, corporate communication is a huge task requiring wide ranging implementation with the primary aim being to communicate the same message to all its stakeholders. Excellent communication orchestrates all internal and external targets to create favorable point-of-view among the goals. All stakeholders on which the target depends have to be involved in the communication. Only an external and neutral coaching approach has the power to manage this exceedingly complex communications process.

Corporate Communications help organizations explain their mission while combining its visions and values into a cohesive message to stakeholders. To be certain of clear target communication, one must know how the message reaches the audience. Feedback from the audience provides the needed information that determines if the mission, vision and values have been communicated. This feedback is normal business for the ITP coach based on continuous communication with the project members and the feedback to management and stakeholders.

The mix of sustainable target definitions, the clear communication and the feedback from the target audience leads to an incomparable team power.

If you are already convinced to be a part of the ITP coach success story, then go to chapter 11 for more information how to participate.

It is always easier to attack and criticize that which is new and innovative. It is much more difficult to be on the cutting edge and learning a new process then implementing that process. But the potential for positive impact is tremendous. Becoming a part of the ITP coaches network offers an easy way to readily dispatch obstacles with a great team power approach that quickly impacts the bottom line.

Summarization of the themes of this chapter:

- Learning the importance of an agile system to generate ongoing positive responses to all past, current and future challenges;
- Understanding that teamwork and the use of collective learning theory provide a path for success;
- Transforming the challenge in hardware and software management by team power and knowledge advantage;
- Recognizing that employees' understanding about company objectives can work against company success;
- Presenting goals clearly and properly so team players pull in the same directions.

9

The Ideal Solution of a Strong Network

The core idea

The core idea of the ITP coach approach is based on the ideal solution of a strong network. The ITP coaches will network among themselves and assist project teams to do the same.

Many of the people you meet at a networking event will be on Facebook, Linkedin, Twitter or some other social networking site. These tools facilitate adventures into networking because a foundation has already been established. However, truly successful networking depends on individual efforts along with the commitment of the person concerned.

The ITP coaches networking possibilities provide a quick and effective foundation to take networking to a quantum level.

Team network advantages among others are:
- Developing confidence and actively participating in a collective learning approach;
- Engaging in confidence-building measures that are focused with trust as the key;
- Providing a value-rich opportunity to achieve high quality learning outcomes;
- Fostering collaboration, as well as competition;
- Focusing on opportunities to give back to the network;
- Bringing together people with differing expertise and different perspectives so that they can grow together;

- Identifying creative and innovative solutions to complex problems;
- Producing group outcomes of a very high standard.

The core, revolutionary idea is that the ITP coaches network is continuously growing in both quantity and quality. Quality increases all the time because IT specialists and excellent coaches operate together in a collective learning approach and share their successes and insights. An interactive exchange of strategies, tactics, challenges, methods, knowledge, skills as well as procedures enhance the best practice portfolio of the members. Each member alternately assumes the position of a supervisor of single members or teams animating the exchange of their activities. The core idea is that there is an intensive give-and-take within the team and within the whole network. This occurs in a friendly, motivationing and creative environment. An additional advantage is the neutrality of ITP coaches, as they work from the network in different companies.

Member principles

The ITP coaches network builds, affirms, demands and practices a code of ethical conduct.

Member principles are:

- Being prepared for a networking event. It's important that the members know: who took part in the last event and what was discussed in the past, in case some questions surface about the topics and issues;
- Asking questions, following the ICF code of ethical conduct. Listen to the response and ask follow-up questions. Weave in some of one's own experiences so the community can learn from it;
- Recognizing and practicing that all ITP coaches have valuable insights to give to their colleagues and that by exercising one's

"giving muscle," all will gain exponentially from the professional relationships;
- Building teleconferences which can be studied and consulted in
retrospection;
- Sending articles or news releases that relate to and add to ongoing conversations or trigger new ones;
- Supervising people with similar backgrounds and work history.

It is an honor to be part of this network and to be able to contribute to the "storehouse of experience and knowledge." This is made
possible by the strong commitment to the vision and the motivating, creative cooperation. The role model of the network, its form
and structure test and reinforce these principles continuously.

The impact of networking

The impact of networking drives managers to develop very strong
links among themselves which subsequently will generate great success for them. Facebook and LinkedIn demonstrate the natural urge
of people to network. If you follow these natural impulses and put
a clear focus on the relevance, it automatically generates success. It
just works.

These days, most people don't have the time for irrelevant conversation. To network effectively, you need to work on something
that's relevant. That means making very clear declarations to the
network members about what you're trying to accomplish, the
implications resulting from success and why all of that is essential
information. From this point, the code of ethical conduct helps to
focus on relevant and clear tasks.

To be effective with a network over the long run, you have to
deliver on your commitments, demonstrate that you have the power
to do so and act with positive intent.

The collective learning approach

The revolutionary collective learning approach generates ambitious benefits:

- Access new and expanding resources to assist your professional development while making learning easier, including new technologies;
- Belong to an organization that continuously builds a leading edge framework;
- Blow up the boundaries of isolated individuality and grow in a collegial network;
- Attend events, conferences, webinars and other learning sessions formed by the collective;
- Have ongoing support in organizing, documenting and evaluating your continuing professional development;
- Participate in a highly motivated collective and learn more rapidly and extensively than in an individual approach;
- Influence the direction of a new and holistic communication system in project management;
- Receive unique opportunities to contribute to a worldwide success story.

Curiosity is the engine of achievement!
Sir Ken Robinson

In the ITP coaches network, members encourage each other in maintaining the curiosity necessary to make every IT project a success. Moreover, the IT coaches network members want their determination for success to support millions of people to be motivated in their own particular work. In the ITP coaches network all members become teachers because they grow together and mutually benefit from each other. In this collective learning approach, the learning power is multiplied with, by and for all members. Each and every member of the ITP coaches network is a mentor who stimulates, provokes and engages. There are no tests in the ITP coaches network to measure member's knowledge and creativity. Instead, collegiality and self-supervision among members provides a kind of diagnosis of the members' abilities. And members know that they can always improve their abilities through the network.

I have mentioned previously my interest in and appreciation of the work of Sir Ken Robinson. This includes the speeches of Sir Ken Robinson which address educational issues in traditional school classrooms. I see these speeches as very easily adaptable to the business world. Currently, in IT projects there exists a culture of compliance. Project Management identifies and adapts strict roles. Project members are encouraged to follow routine algorithms rather than attempt to ignite their powers of imagination and curiosity. This is a common and perhaps the easiest method to manage a project team. However, the easiest way is not necessarily the best way. An important statement from Sir Ken Robinson is that human life is inherently creative:

". . . we create lives, and we can recreate them as we go through them. It's the common currency of being a human being. It's why human culture is so interesting and diverse and dynamic."

He states also: "One of the roles of education is to awaken and develop these powers of creativity."

In the IT world there is a culture of standardization, but in my professional experience, I have discovered that often only curiosity, creativity and improvisation lead to success. The ITP coaches network is comprised of interesting, diverse and dynamic individuals who thrive on creativity and improvisation. These factors form the foundation of its quality. This ensures in a very simple way that the ITP coach recognizes clearly what is requested: the standard approach or an approach that expects improvisation. With this awareness, the ITP coach provides the requisite goal-oriented assistance. The ITP coach approach supports the project management in distinguishing when standardization is necessary or when creativity and improvisation are to be implemented.

"Investing in professional development is not a cost, it's an investment!"

This statement from Sir Ken Robinson describes the ITP coaches network. Each network member holds responsibility to successfully implement the collective learning approach. This strong commitment is key to be part of the success story. The ITP coaches are highly motivated and committed to actively engage curiosity and creativity, and to help grow an important part of our society. We have to fine tune mechanisms in our world, not merely adapt industrial standardization. The ITP coaching connects various constructive, creative and effective approaches. In today's diverse and dynamic IT project teams we need a very flexible and adaptive ITP coach approach!

I encourage you to watch on TED the speech by Sir Ken Robinson outlining the 3 crucial principles to make the human mind flourish:

http://www.ted.com/talks/ken_robinson_how_to_escape_education_s_death_valley.html

The symbiosis of being able to grow professionally in the network and then to be able to apply the new knowledge and understanding in the job has various positive synergies. A coach working for an IT project will be paid by hours or working days. For certified ITP coaches the time devoted in the network represents an investment in education and supervision along with the general benefits derived from networking. As a matter of course, certified ITP coaches significantly increase their personal skills. When professional ITP coaches engage in projects in different companies, the network benefits through the expansion and diversity of the working scope.

Through the ITP coaches network, members have access to other professionals with similar skill sets as well as those with vastly different skill sets. This provides individuals with unique opportunities to learn new skills or to reinforce current ones. Each ITP coach approaches every project with a solid foundation of knowledge and with the awareness that if the coach encounters problems, he has the network to turn to for guidance, advice and support. So this increases the potential for IT projects to come in on time and on budget. Success generates success generates success which establishes a motivating creative framework for extraordinary performance. The passion of the network members intensifies the drive for continuous growth. To be part of a Trillion Dollar IT Revolution and helping motivate thousands of IT employees is pure passion!

> *Educating the mind without educating the heart*
> *is no education at all.*
> Quote credited to Aristotle (384 BC–322 BC) the Greek philosopher

Collective learning goes "viral" in a highly motivated community. The ITP coaches network is a highly motivated community. Members participate with their hearts and minds—passion and knowledge—in order to benefit the whole. Members holding in common a drive to make each IT project a success is highly motivating, not only for the involved companies but also for the involved people. There are millions of users of IT systems which can benefit from this success.

Motivation, creativity and passion are the ingredients by which the collective learning prescription stanches the bleeding wounds of failed IT projects in order to heal IT projects. Like a doctor, I advise taking the medication as soon as possible to the benefit of IT projects health. This enables the involved firms to save a large amount of money and time and makes them significantly reduce burn-outs and loss of motivation.

Rules of intelligence

How do we combine and multiply intelligence in a wining network? Sometimes the emotional body dominates the intellect and generates challenges in the project team. In such situations, the ITP coach must intervene, as he represents a neutral person outside the line organization.

People tend to learn by heart certain things that others do not. Negative childhood experiences can trigger emotional blocks in us as adults which result in our inability to learn a process or concept. But the same extant emotional blockages may arise in a project team. Maybe an experienced programmer laughs repeatedly about the script errors of a colleague. In a coaching session such an offending constellation can be detected and resolved. The impact of emotions is an underestimated factor in teamwork. High performance teamwork is only possible in an emotionally safe and balanced environment.

There are other challenges to solve in the emotional intelligence arena. Normally individuals in projects function from solution-oriented perspectives. When emotions emerge, barriers appear. Taking the IT project to completion is no longer the main objective.

Such emotional situations often play out on the relationship level. Team members who once worked well together now may argue or disagree. This may lead to confusing confrontations. Questions like "What does this person have against me?" often lead to interpersonal conflicts. However, even worse than the disagreement is ignoring the situation; simply choosing to not deal with it. If emotional issues remain unaddressed, they expand unconsciously in a negative spiral. Emotions assume power over the intellect. Things get overstated. It's crucial for ITP coaches to apply a coaching approach to prevent those situations.

Not only does the project team benefit from an emotional balanced atmosphere, but also the ITP coaches network takes advantage of it. In the rapidly changing and growing computer science environment one encounters more and more intellectual limits while the pace of change is accelerating. Today, computers exceed human intelligence in a wide variety of arenas like playing chess or forecasting the weather. Human intelligence overall remains far more agile and flexible. In the collective learning approach the ITP coaches network will highly benefit from this flexibility.

Individuals generally learn in a linear way. When something occurs to disrupt the linear learning process, blockades and barriers appear. People who are able to grow in another way through the collective learning approach will quickly move beyond the barriers and blockades to cooperation and team work. Venturing into the physical world and sharing knowledge with each other is already a big advantage, a gift of human beings.

The combination of human-level intelligence with a computer's inherent superiority of speed, accuracy, and sharing of its memory is formidable. The symbiosis strengthens and sustains a highly motivating network. That effectively utilizes each individual team member in a friendly environment. This is the revolutionary way of the ITP coaches network.

The ITP coaches network is not subject to competition. One of the highest priorities in the network is to promote other members in supervision. It is thus comparable to a continuous *lessons learned* meeting. The collective learning approach has profound implications for all aspects of human endeavor, including the work life balance, human learning and the concept of ourselves. As IT is one of the biggest businesses in our economic world it also possesses a large application field. Therefore, members of the ITP coaches network are highly motivated to be part of, maintain and grow this unprecedented, revolutionary approach.

Most of the improvements that could make us smarter would hit limits set by the laws of physics. Various researches suggest that human intelligence may be close to its evolutionary limit. However, applying the collective learning approach, humans might still achieve greater awareness, knowledge and understanding. The framework of the ITP coaches network enables to expand the mind outside the confines of our body.

Sometimes it seems that the evolution process has forgotten human communication skills. In the pre-Christian era of the Greek philosophers, the communication culture was far more advanced than in many parts of the world today. It is important to be attentive that the same does not happen to our intellectual skills. We have to combine IQ with EQ. The emotional quotient (EQ) or emotional intelligence refers to the ability to perceive, control and evaluate emotions. For good communication skills it's appropriate to control emotions. Since 1990, Peter Salovey and John D. Mayer have been the leading researchers on emotional intelligence. In their influential article "Emotional Intelligence," they defined emotional intelligence as:

"The subset of social intelligence that involves the ability to monitor one's own and others' feelings and emotions, to discriminate among them and to use this information to guide one's thinking and actions."

This principal looks like a medieval practice of fighting an enemy and speaks for an evolutionary step backwards. It's important that we continue to evolve, to recognize harmful behavior and to address it. The ITP coaches network is the ideal mechanism for this.

Social competence, emotional intelligence and soft skills are very important in today's business world. It's a multifaceted concept consisting of social, emotional and behavioral soft skills as well as motivational anticipation sets needed for successful social adaptation. Another reflection of these skills is having an ability to take another's perspective concerning a situation and to learn from past experiences. The ITP coach applies that learning to the changes in social interactions. This is the foundation upon which successful opportunities for future interaction with others is built.

An ITP coach with a high emotional intelligence and social competence is able to recognize their own emotional state and the emotional states of others, and engage with people in a very positive and motivating way. They can use this understanding of emotions to relate better to other people, form healthier relationships, achieve greater success at work, and lead a more fulfilling work-life balance.

The ability to identify, practice, understand and handle emotions in positive ways to eliminate stress, communicate effectively, empathize with others, overcome challenges and resolve conflicts describes the essential skill set of an ITP coach.

With the collective learning approach, these great skill sets will be quickly propagated across the ITP coaches network.

There are other holistic concepts around intelligence. We possess a physical body, an emotional body and an intellectual body. They can be conflicted or complementary. The collective learning process provides perfect support to deal properly with all personal skills.

I learned on the pilgrimage route to Santiago how important it is to let thoughts flow into the physical intelligence. After a few days of meditative walking, I felt my intuition taking its natural place again. Many great thinkers of human history attained groundbreaking inspirations through meditation, inner peace or breaks. As an example, Albert Einstein conceived the theory of relativity while riding his bicycle. The reason may be that in relaxed situations the brain is not "overheated" and can perceive holistic inputs again. As in a laboratory, ITP coaches can grow with these experiences and the resulting knowledge in their own network. During the stakes in IT projects, the acquired knowledge can be implemented and grow. The creativity of the ITP coaches network and the stability of the implementation in the business are a winning relationship.

Analogies to sports

In golf, the first shot on each hole is critical. Also for an ITP coach it's important to start with the period in which the business case will be scheduled. Golf is one of the few ball games that does not require a standardized playing area. Also an ITP coach is deployable in various environments. Each hole on the course must contain a "tee box" to start from and a "putting green" with the actual hole. For an

ITP coach there are various other standardized forms, procedures or methods to ensure compliance with. The ITP coaches network builds a certification committee to grant compliance in their profession. This routine to create rules makes the network grow and flourish.

The sailing trophy "America's Cup" was renamed after the first winning yacht and was donated to the New York Yacht Club (NYYC) under the terms of the Deed of Gift, which made the cup available for perpetual international competition. The winning approach of the ITP coaches network is building its own terms which makes the idea available for a worldwide success story.

Another great example of the winning spirit of the ITP coaches network is the $1,000,000 question to promote greater or stronger team power. If you ask a team what they would do with $1,000,000 in a lonely place, suddenly creativity flourishes and motivation abounds. And there are further wonderful and powerful approaches to continue to promote the strength of the network team. On www.itpcoach.com/08 are a few more examples of motivational tools. The network is like a brotherhood, to sail, play golf and implement world-class professionalism in one unit.

Summarization of the themes of this chapter:

- The core idea of the advantages of a strong network and team network;
- The network member principles of continually building a code of ethical conduct;
- The impact of Networking effectively on something that's relevant;
- The different benefits that the revolutionary collective learning approach will grant;
- The varieties of "intelligence" and how to combine and multiply them in a winning network;
- The comparisons from the world of sports.

10

The ITP Coach Association,
the Framework for the Network

Trust is basic

Trust is the grease that makes any network successful. Any interested company can designate one or more persons whom the company knows to be trustworthy for inclusion in the network. This establishes from the beginning the absolute requirement of strong trust by, for, with and among the members of the network. This element of trust will grow stronger as the network expands and the framework of the organization molds into shape.

Quality of service (QoS) is only one aspect of the framework for the ITP coaches network. Best practice knowledge of the ITP coach association members combined with the collective learning approach will undergird continual growth of an excellent technical framework.

Other significant elements of the network framework include excellent communication skills, a solid commitment to the network and a high degree of personal motivation, the will and vision to work collegially and engage in important, holistic missions which allow members to soar to new professional and socially responsible heights.

Both the network and the framework will develop according to the latest standards and leading edge technologies.

The IT revolution is based on the trust in the technology—and—in the people involved.

The best way to find out if you can trust somebody is to trust them.
Ernest Hemingway

In the ITP coaches network it makes sense that trust develops gradually, allowing people time to assess the trustworthiness of others. The strong commitment and the motivation to be part of this encourage members to quickly adopt and practice Ernest Hemingway's comment about trust.

In establishing trust within the ITP coaches network subliminal hints are used, such as the name of a good friend held in common, to create feelings of trust. Focusing on establishing trust helps explain the good vibes we sometimes immediately pick up from strangers. The vision and goals of *The Trillion Dollar IT Revolution* are grounded in establishing and maintaining the feelings of trust. With trust established, the ITP coaches trust each other to fulfill their roles, although they may have little experience working together. This internal trust is built over time, eventually leading to confidence within and among one another.

With confidence, you have won before you have started.
Marcus Garvey

Successful formation

The members of the network are composed of brilliant IT specialists and splendid coaches. This will guarantee a high technical and a high communication standard for the framework.

Clear, concrete, correct, coherent and effective communication and appropriate, agile, accessible, ambitious and visionary technical skills are combined in this framework.

All of those attributes will result in excellent solutions that demonstrate the success of the ITP coach approach and will provide an ever growing resource of unforgettable success stories.

The successful formation of the framework starts with coaches from networks sourcing on strategic alliances. Many of them have profound IT experience. Some have worked for decades in IT before their coaching career. These founding members will generate the framework.

Interested companies are invited to designate a person of trust for membership in the network. These reliable people will play critical roles in helping the network to grow and flourish. A two-step-approach to membership in the ITP coaches network is discussed in the next chapter.

Proof of concept

The idea of the framework is that transmission rates, error rates, and other characteristics can be measured, improved, and, to some extent, guaranteed in advance. Another goal is to create and maintain an ongoing system of professional success and mutual benefit.

Members of the framework can communicate together worldwide under the best possible conditions. This is guaranteed by the mix of brilliant IT professionals and splendid coaches. By focusing on creativity, motivation and excellent skills, network members will establish this leading edge framework for the ITP coaches network.

A proof of concept (POC) is a realization of a certain method or idea to verify that some concept or theory has the potential of being used. A proof of concept is usually small and may or may not be complete. In contrast to this definition, the POC of the framework for the ITP coaches network is based on an initial workshop as a huge and unique experiment. During this initial workshop, interested IT specialists and coaches, as well as all founding members, expand upon the design of the framework.

All the ideals of this vision—this IT revolution—will be explained, discussed and implemented in the founding workshop.

The output of the workshop will be documented in audio and video information products as well as teleseminars to provide facts to interested prospects.

This approach of initiating the ITP coaches network will prove the concept and bring together a highly motivated group of specialists to build the extraordinary high tech framework.

Makes a difference

If you ask a room full of coaches to define the art of coaching and what it means to them, you're almost certain to get as many different answers as there are people present. Coaching is an interesting business. Everyone seems to have a different take on it. According to a 2007 *MarketData* study, an estimated 40,000 people in the US work as business or life coaches. Coaching is a $2.4 billion industry and grows at the rate of 18% per year. Some people feel that having a main career at which they are successful will help lend some credibility to their claim of being a good coach.

One factor for the rapidly growing number of working coaches might be that there's not a lot of turnover in the industry. A full 85% of coaches indicate that they intend to stay in this field for at least a decade. The Professional Business Coach Alliance, The International Coach Federation ICF, the International Coaching Council and the Worldwide Association of Business Coaches provide membership-based associations for business coaching professionals. Those and other organizations train professionals to offer business coaching to business owners.

Business coaching offers personal support and feedback and combines a coaching approach with practical and structured business planning. This style of coaching brings a disciplined accountability to the relationship. The coaching process is as concerned about driving profit as it is about developing the person. According to the National Post, business coaching is one of the fastest growing industries in the world.

The difference between business coaching and ITP coaching is the network and collective learning approach in a special market niche—the IT projects. Coaching in general is a business with a lot of niche areas for the specialist. The ITP coaches network addresses a very specific niche/profession. The difference between coaching and the ITP coaches network is significant.

Growing together is key in the framework and the collective learning approach will facilitate reaching this goal. The mix of the manifold skills of the network members combined with their work in different IT projects all around the world will enhance the power of the framework. This power will be multiplied through the collective learning approach.

The power of a pool approach

The pool approach highly influences the world of employment. Physically the pool is a known group of people undertaking an actual set of working tasks within the workplace. Pools have a number of very significant advantages to staff development. In multinationals and big IT companies there exist different working pools for dedicated working groups. Specialized pools can be found for project managers, business analysts and software specialists. Pools are economical, easy to establish and manage, and they build teams and your business while developing the individual. The goal is to develop people not only for one specific job but also to develop a broad skill set in each person so that a pool member is ready to take on several possible positions. The value is twofold: employees get to work in projects they would normally never have access to—this is exciting, challenging and valuable. Secondly, the business has at its disposal many people who are good at many things—the strategic and operational benefits are evident. Building robust working pools is not a "nice to have," but a necessity to create and sustain competitive advantage.

The ITP coaches network clearly supports this pool approach with integrated collective learning to develop members' skills. As part of this pool, the ITP coach works in different projects using different synergies and comes to an agreement with stakeholders to select the highest value work assignment.

Globalization, demographic shifts, differing expectations of generations, the demand for transparency, and the freedom of choice about where and when to work are just some of the issues forcing multinationals to reconsider how they acquire and manage their specialists. As the world becomes a smaller place and as businesses continue to expand their global footprint, the need for a holistic approach and the ability to access quality local specialists is a key success criterion. Companies now understand that they need to invest in building and managing global pools to create a real and sustainable competitive advantage.

The framework of the ITP coaches network is a global pool, a community of qualified specialists who are actively interested in your organization and your success and are engaged over time to bring IT projects to the road of success.

Strategic alliances

In addition there are so many great networks to combine with the power of coaching.

In the *Stakeholder Centered Coaching* network by Marshall Goldsmith there are more than 750 coaches worldwide, working together for guaranteed and measurable leadership growth. The ITP coaches network can learn from their network abilities and in return support from a deeper contact with the base of employees. Merged, these two coaching methods result in a coaching power from top down and bottom up: a really 360-degree approach.

In human resources or general bonus qualification systems, 360-degree feedback, also known as multi source feedback, is feedback that comes from employees, subordinates and stakeholders. The results from a 360-degree evaluation are often used by the persons receiving the feedback to plan and map specific paths in their growth.

The ITP coaches network, the *Stakeholder Centered Coaching* network and all involved companies together can benefit from this holistic feedback.

The *Stakeholder Centered Coaching* by Marshall Goldsmith (SCC-MG) enables successful leaders to achieve positive and measurable change in leadership behavior. It's a system for continuous improvement for themselves and their teams. This approach focuses one a top down view by including the stakeholders of the involved leaders and the impact their teams have. The ITP coach works close to the project teams and rapports to leaders and stakeholders, a typical bottom up approach. As the coach operates from an observer view the SCC-MG and ITP coach approach combined, open new different, holistic views to the companies working environment.

If in a SCC-MG coaching a goal set by the leadership is to improve employee motivation, productivity and performance, this is congruent with the ITP coach approach. Also the executive coach is able to clearly communicate the leadership goals to the ITP coach. Then the ITP coach grants the clear communication to the project team. This is a high quality combination of two success stories.

If you are interested in receiving more information about the combination of the *Stakeholder Centered Coaching* by Marshall Goldsmith (SCC-MG) and the ITP coach approach, then go to www.itpcoach.com/09.

Summarization of the themes of this chapter:
- The importance of trust in building the framework of the ITP coaches network;
- The successful formation of the framework;
- The review of the concept of coaching;
- The difference the network and the collective learning approach provides in a special market niche;
- The Pool approach highly influences the world of employment;
- The strong tool that emerges when coaching approaches are combined.

11

How to Join the Winning Team

Building a network

I firmly believe that the building of a network is a very individual and deliberate process. I have a large network in which people trust me. Our shared experiences and encounters have always demonstrated that they can trust me. We maintain confidence in each other's abilities, knowledge, reliability and trustworthiness. The process to build the ITP coaches network is generic and is based on strategic alliances.

I intend to promote the idea of the ITP coaches network in order to integrate the power of trust into the ITP coach community. This concern for establishing and maintaining trust within, between and among members is why I prefer a two-step approach to enter in the ITP coaches network. If the ITP coaches network is formed and equipped with super motivated specialists who possess strong self-confidence, this generic and situational approach to build a network promises the greatest chance of achievement for a long term success story.

The two-step approach to enter in the network

If you are convinced that your business in general and the IT segment of your business in particular will benefit by utilizing an ITP coach in your IT project management, then designate a person of trust for membership in the network. This person will enter as a passive member of the ITP coaches network and participate in specific meetings. In this way, your representative and your business can establish a clear understanding of and confidence in the role of an ITP coaches network. In addition, the investment for the passive membership is relatively moderate. If the person feels comfortable in the network and is convinced of the benefits of membership, the next step is to become an active membership.

This two-step approach provides prospective members with:

- The opportunity to approach the issue step by step;
- Proof that the network can regulate itself and grow sustainably;
- Participation in a revolutionary collective learning approach while building it;
- A return on your investment through benefits by improving your practice in a top network;
- Satisfaction in peer recognition and networking opportunities;
- Help to advance members' careers, showcase their expertise, support their development and advance their specialty ITP coach education.

These several positive effects of the two-step approach in becoming first a passive and then an active member you are designed to motivate you want to be part of this success story.

Explore the eligibility requirements and benefits of active membership. Join, use and expand the network, connect with your colleagues, and give your specialty a voice. An active membership supports the foundation of the network and brings experience to the network idea, as described in this book, to make a breakthrough in IT project success.

The key mission of the ITP coaches network is to build and to maintain strong member skills. These emotionally balanced strengths help the whole vision to break through and secure the ability of the ITP coaches to optimally support IT project teams.

Active members get access to the following ingredients for successful results, the ability to:

1. develop mature skills, to better understand, manage, negotiate with and lead other people;
2. effectively read others and react appropriately to shift from leadership style to leadership tactic;
3. establish self-awareness by tuning in to true feelings, motivations, aptitudes and limitations;
4. demonstrate self-regulation by taking responsibility, handling change with flexibility and being open to new ideas;
5. manage self-control by managing emotions effectively to face challenges balanced and focused;
6. build confidence by maintaining standards of honesty and integrity;
7. create motivational skills by constant striving to improve, aligning with goals despite obstacles and setbacks;
8. be service oriented by anticipating, recognizing and meeting clients' needs;
9. sense what others need to progress and bolstering their abilities;
10. leverage diversity by cultivating opportunities through diverse people;
11. grow political awareness and comprehension by discerning the feelings behind the needs and wants of others;
12. realize communication and leadership skills by sending clear messages, inspiring, guiding groups and people;
13. establish conflict management by understanding, negotiating and resolving disagreements;
14. work toward shared goals and create group synergy in pursuing collective targets.

The target of this best practice by ITP coaches is to continuously realign IT projects and their members' activities to realize a final "touch down." As a network, members will be diligent in locating the weak links in the IT deliverable chain to improve processes accordingly.

This process can be easely demonstrated by a picture:

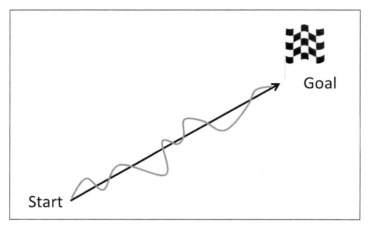

Illustration 8: Permanent feedback and realigning system of the success story

On the NASA flight to the moon the direction (line between start and goal) was very clear and visible. Based upon data and analysis generated by the astronauts and ground support, corrections were carried out permanently during the perpetual flight to the moon. Only with the ITP coach process are these kinds of realignments in your IT projects possible.

- Develop teamwork spirit to build highly effective task-forces and eliminate frustration and increase people's work quality;
- Strategize project management with the new ITP Coaching process to receive the results you want and differentiate yourself significantly from every competitor in the IT market;
- Build confidence between IT and Business to produce opti-mized solutions;
- Create a realistic, true communication flow between IT projects and stakeholders.

Through strategic alliances and joint ventures, the basis for the ITP coaches network is established with members of coach networks that already exist.

Join this ITP Coaches Network now, rescue a lot of money and time by creating your unique IT success story!

To find out the status of the active ITP coaches network, please go to www.itpcoach.com/10.

Summarization of the themes of this chapter:

- Identifying and sending a person of trust for participation in the network;
- Recognizing several positive effects of the two step approach in becoming an active member.

Index

About the Author

URS MILZ knows Multinational's IT business from top to bottom. He sees the large picture in order to optimize processes, communication and strategies. Be it programming, testing, quality or project management, Urs possesses extraordinary knowledge. As an experienced Senior Consultant, business analyst, project leader and professional Coach, he consistently demonstrates his ability in knowing how to lead IT projects to success. Along his career, Urs gained extensive experience in cultivating opportunities and resolving disagreements. With insightful, emotional intelligence, he builds confidence and group synergies to produce optimized solutions. Urs dedicates his professional expertise in IT project management to Multinationals—improving processes and work quality. His new, unique ITP Coach Process defines best practices of leadership and communication to achieve success in today's IT world.